Walking with Wildflowers

9/5/94

D0147380

Walking

with

Wildflowers

A Field Guide to the St. Louis Area

Karen S. Haller

University of Missouri Press   Columbia and London

Library of Congress Cataloging-in-Publication Data

Haller, Karen S., 1935–

    Walking with wildflowers : a field guide to the St.
  Louis area / Karen S. Haller.

        p.   cm.

  Includes bibliographical references (p.   ) and index.

  ISBN 0-8262-0950-5 (paper)

  1. Wild flowers–Missouri–Saint Louis Region–
  Identification.

  I. Title.

  QK170.H25   1994

  582.13'09778'65—dc20   93-48414

                                         CIP

Designer: Kristie Lee
Printer and binder: Dai Nippon
Typeface: Adobe™ Minion

Maps prepared by John M. Kennington.
All photographs are by Karen S. Haller with the exception of
the following: Yellow Crownbeard and Ironweed, Jim
Bogler; Goat's Rue, Arthur Christ; Giant Forget-me-not,
John Molyneaux.

To Arthur Christ, my friend of many years, patient botanical mentor, and able adviser. The depth of his knowledge of Missouri's flora, his consummate skill in recognizing the local flora in the field, and his enthusiastic attitude expressed when sharing this wisdom with others encouraged thousands of individuals to become interested in wildflowers.

Generous with his time, he served as a voluntary leader of wildflower walks for both the Webster Groves Nature Study Society and the Missouri Botanical Garden. His infectious, gentle humor brightened each expedition.

I had hoped to be able to work with him through the entire process of creating and publishing this book. His unexpected death on February 17, 1991, ended this possibility. Upon his death, I made a promise to myself and to Arthur's sister, Adele, to finish this book and to dedicate it to Arthur. It took three more years to fulfill that promise. Surely Arthur would be pleased and proud of this achievement.

Contents

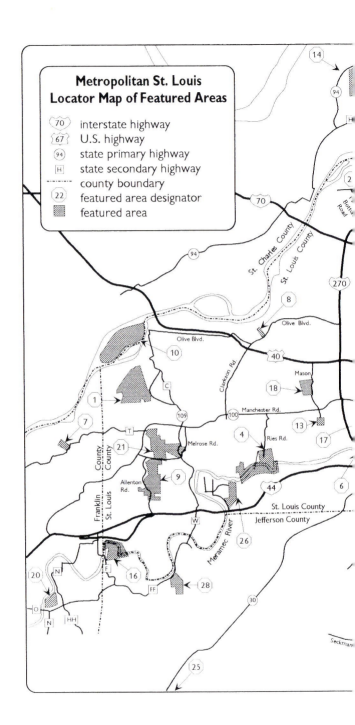

Metropolitan St. Louis
Locator Map of Featured Areas

- 70   interstate highway
- 67   U.S. highway
- 94   state primary highway
- H   state secondary highway
- ·····   county boundary
- 22   featured area designator
- ▨   featured area

St. Charles County
St. Louis County

Olive Blvd.

Mason

Manchester Rd.

Melrose Rd.

Ries Rd.

Allenton Rd.

Clarkson Rd.

County County
Franklin St. Louis

St. Louis County
Jefferson County

Meramec River

Bottom Road

Seckman

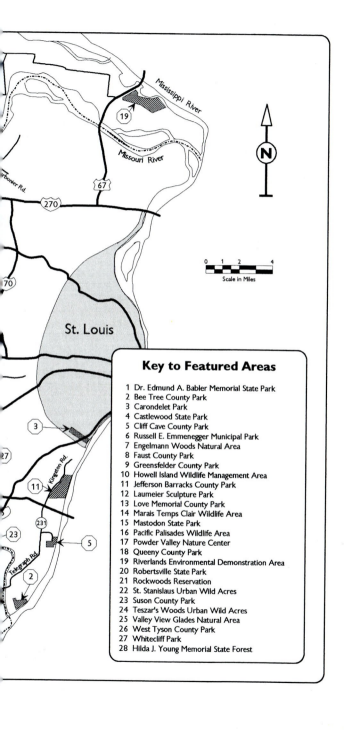

Mississippi River

Missouri River

⑲

⬆
N

〔67〕

〔270〕

〔70〕

0 1 2 4
Scale in Miles

St. Louis

③

〔27〕

⑪

〔231〕

㉓

⑤

Kingston Rd.

Telegraph Rd.

②

Key to Featured Areas

1 Dr. Edmund A. Babler Memorial State Park
2 Bee Tree County Park
3 Carondelet Park
4 Castlewood State Park
5 Cliff Cave County Park
6 Russell E. Emmenegger Municipal Park
7 Engelmann Woods Natural Area
8 Faust County Park
9 Greensfelder County Park
10 Howell Island Wildlife Management Area
11 Jefferson Barracks County Park
12 Laumeier Sculpture Park
13 Love Memorial County Park
14 Marais Temps Clair Wildlife Area
15 Mastodon State Park
16 Pacific Palisades Wildlife Area
17 Powder Valley Nature Center
18 Queeny County Park
19 Riverlands Environmental Demonstration Area
20 Robertsville State Park
21 Rockwoods Reservation
22 St. Stanislaus Urban Wild Acres
23 Suson County Park
24 Teszar's Woods Urban Wild Acres
25 Valley View Glades Natural Area
26 West Tyson County Park
27 Whitecliff Park
28 Hilda J. Young Memorial State Forest

Walking with Wildflowers

Introduction

The intent of this guide, with its emphasis on where to find selected species of wildflowers, is to provide assistance to both the novice and the advanced botanist in the recognition and appreciation of the flora of St. Louis. Since 1977, Arthur Christ and I have regularly traversed the trails of Missouri's state and local parks, Department of Conservation–owned lands, and other botanically interesting sites in search of wildflowers in bloom. With the information accumulated from these trips, I filled notebook after notebook. Finally, Arthur and I decided to share this wealth of information by organizing it into a simple, down-to-earth field guide for use by individuals interested in planning their own wildflower walks.

Twenty-eight areas within an hour's drive of St. Louis are featured in this volume. Included are three municipal parks, ten St. Louis County parks, four state parks, ten Missouri Department of Conservation–owned lands, and one U.S. Army Corps of Engineers area. An opening page for each area gives its name, the acreage and location by county, directions for reaching the entrance, information on the visitor center (if there is one), and a designation of ownership with a telephone number to call for additional information. Facing the opening page for each area is a map pinpointing the location of each of the wildflowers featured for that area. In addition, the Locator Map of Featured Areas indicates the location of all twenty-eight areas in relation to each other and to the city of St. Louis.

A total of seventy diverse wildflowers are featured, of which sixty-one are native to Missouri. The description of each plant begins with a heading identifying both its common name and its scientific name. Two sources have been used as authorities: *Flora of Missouri* (1963) by Julian A. Steyermark and *Catalogue*

1

of the Flora of Missouri (1990) by George Yatskievych and Joanna Turner. When two scientific names are given, as in *Seymeria macrophylla (Dasistoma macrophylla)*, the first is from Steyermark and the second, in parentheses, is from Yatskievych and Turner. Further notations specify the native or introduced status of each species and indicate whether it is perennial, biennial, or annual. Finally, the blooming months for each wildflower are given as designated in Steyermark's *Flora of Missouri*. Because these dates are for the entire state of Missouri rather than specific to the St. Louis area, they are followed by the date, in parentheses, when that particular flower is most likely to be found in bloom in the area in which it is featured. This information has been determined from blooming-date records compiled for sixteen years. One week on either side of this date, depending on the weather patterns of a particular year, should provide the greatest potential for successful in-bloom sightings.

More detailed descriptions provide information on the color, texture, and measurements of each plant, focusing on the stem, flower, and leaves. Plant measurements are given in millimeters, centimeters, or meters. A millimeter (mm) is one-tenth of a centimeter. One centimeter (cm) is equal to 0.39 inch. There are 100 centimeters in a meter (m), which is thus the equivalent of 39.97 inches, or just over one yard. Measurements given for each featured wildflower have been taken in the field, from dried specimens in the herbarium of Art Christ, or from species housed at the Missouri Botanical Garden Herbarium. Descriptions of flowers include only the most noticeable features, primarily the petals and sepals. Reproductive parts are referred to if of a particularly interesting shape, color, or length. Failure to describe them does not mean they are missing. To assist in immediate visual identification in the field, the description of each wildflower is accompanied by a color photograph on the facing page.

Written descriptions of each species's location supplement the designations on the area maps, whenever possible using specific compass directions and mileage measurements. The distance given at the end of each *Location* paragraph refers to the distance to and among the featured flowers; it is not for a

Walking with Wildflowers

round trip. Distances are measured in English units, rather than in metric, because most maps and pedometers still use these units of measure. It will help in interpreting the directions to know that there are 1,760 yards in a mile, or 220 yards to an eighth of a mile, which is rendered in decimal units as 0.125 mile. Finally, detailed information regarding the trail surface and difficulty is provided, along with any cautionary notes that will help to make the reader's search for the wildflower a more pleasant one.

For those wishing to know what flowers might be in bloom at any particular time, the Monthly Schedule at the back of the book lists the featured wildflowers in the order in which they bloom in the St. Louis area. From the list of estimated peak-blooming dates from March through November, the reader can determine which flowers are most likely to be in bloom at any given time and which areas to visit to see those flowers.

Following the Monthly Schedule, the Checklist of plants to be seen at each of the featured areas offers a guide to locating wildflowers other than the featured species. Although the checklist is admittedly limited because of space restrictions, it should be helpful to any wildflower enthusiast looking for places to see particular species. Best of all, it can be personalized by one's own additions.

Following the Checklist, scientific terms that could be unfamiliar are defined in the section sensibly titled Botanical Terms. For those desiring additional information on the wildflowers that can be found in the St. Louis area, References of Interest provides bibliographical information on other works.

With the information provided in this book, the reader can plan successful field trips tailored to his or her schedule, interests, and physical ability. Here are just a few of the possibilities:

Select by Wildflower Photograph

Example: You are thumbing through the book and are overcome by the intensity of color in the Butterfly Weed. You simply have to see it. No problem. On the page facing the photograph is the information regarding location, blooming date, distance to walk from the nearest parking lot, and the trail surface. Jot the blooming date onto your personal daily calendar for a visit at the appropriate time.

Select by Monthly Schedule

Example: You were born in July and receive *Walking with Wildflowers* as a birthday gift. To find out which flowers might be in bloom that week, turn to the Monthly Schedule for a listing of the featured wildflowers that bloom in July, such as the Gum Plant and American Lotus. Turn to the areas indicated by number in the schedule for the text providing all the necessary information for a successful visit.

Select by Featured Areas in the Table of Contents

Example: Scanning the Contents you notice that area 7 is a place called Engelmann Woods Natural Area that features flowers named Celandine Poppy, Leaf-cup, and White Trillium. Your curiosity is aroused. Where is this place? By looking at the Locator Map of Featured Areas you can see that it is in Franklin County, and by turning to the text for area 7, you find directions for reaching the park's entrance. The information on the exact location of the wildflowers in the area, their blooming dates, and how to reach them enables you to plan to explore this newly discovered area.

Select by Geographic Area

Example: Your home territory is St. Charles County. A gadget for your house necessitates a trip to a specialty store in Arnold. It seems like a long way to go just for one item. Enhance the trip by checking the Locator Map of Featured Areas and discovering that Teszar's Woods Urban Wild Acres is in the Arnold area. Throw your hiking boots into the car. Brighten your day with an informative botany hike.

Select by Personal Physical Limitations

Example: Recent surgery on your right foot has limited your physical capability. You are ready now for some exercise but cannot handle uneven terrain. By checking the *Terrain* and *Location* sections of the text you discover that the Tanglevine

Trail at Powder Valley Nature Center is flat, nearly six feet wide, and asphalt covered. You decide to walk the Tanglevine Trail to see the wildflowers growing there.

Select by Checklist

Example: You are a seasoned student of wildflower study, have advanced to using scientific names, and have already seen all the Bluebells and Trout Lilies you have ever wished to see. *Blephilia ciliata* (Ohio Horse Mint), for example, is on your list of plants to see and photograph. A glance at the Checklist reveals eight areas in which it has been known to grow. Check Steyermark's *Flora of Missouri* for needed information, then set off on your own exploration.

As you undertake your search for wildflowers, remember that the natural world is an ever-changing entity full of unexpected surprises—some devastating, some delightful. The conditions described herein are subject to change, both by man and by nature, although every effort has been made to insure that the information provided is as accurate as possible.

Finally, the purchase of a magnifying hand lens, an inexpensive compass, and a simple pedometer could prove beneficial for the most complete use of the book. Walking with a friend is suggested both for companionship and for safety. Enjoy the walk. Enjoy the wildflowers. It's a winning combination.

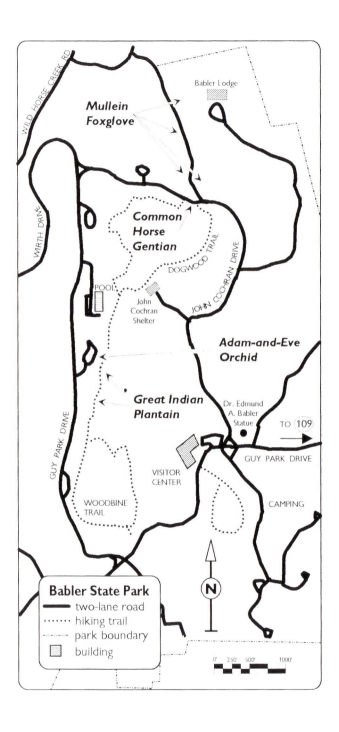

Dr. Edmund A. Babler Memorial State Park

2,439 acres, St. Louis County

Entrance on Highway 109, 4 miles north of Manchester Road (Highway 100), in Chesterfield

River Hills Visitor Center (314–458–3813)

Missouri Department of Natural Resources

Aplectrum hyemale
Orchidaceae
Native biennial
May–June (May 11)

Adam-and-Eve Orchid

Orchid family

Stem Erect, 15 to 40 cm tall, and leafless.

Flower Eight to twenty individual flowers, each 1–1.5 cm long with petals and sepals pale green at the base and purple toward the tip. The lip area is white with purple streaks.

Leaves A single leaf at the base of each plant is dark green, elliptical, and corrugated, 7–20 cm long and 4–9 cm wide with numerous white veins, each extending the full length of the leaf. The leaves are seen most easily in winter but usually disappear by flowering time; search for them from mid-November until April. Seventeen have been seen here.

Location Along Woodbine Trail. Enter the park on Guy Park Drive and continue for 2.1 miles. Turn right at the sign for the Nature Trail Parking Area and park in the northeast corner of the lot, near the wooden bulletin board. Walk southeast on the entrance trail for 15 yards, then right (south) on Woodbine Trail for 30–40 yards. Turn to face the parking lot. Look 2.5 to 3 yards into the greenery for the Adam-and-Eve Orchid. Distance: 58 yards.

Terrain Trail is packed earth with some gravel, basically level, and 2–3 feet wide.

Boarding Pass

Sun Country Airlines

This is a one way seat assignment.
Please present to gate agent for boarding.

22B

Triosteum perfoliatum
Caprifoliaceae
Native perennial
May–July (May 20)

Common Horse Gentian

Honeysuckle family

Stem Erect, up to 1.2 m tall, and hairy, with a mixture of gland-tipped and nonglandular hairs of various lengths.

Flower Corolla tubular to 2 cm long and with the upper edge incised to form five shallow, rounded lobes; apricot to red maroon in color. Also noticeable is the pistil extending 2–3 mm below the tube. Five slender sepals surround the corolla. Individual flowers, ranging in number from one to six, appear at the leaf axils and seem to open in sequence up the stem.

Leaves Opposite, with several pairs of leaves united at the base and thus encircling the stem; somewhat fiddle-shaped and 7–20 cm long by 3–7 cm wide; softly hairy on the underside.

Fruit Orange, round, and 8–10 mm in diameter. Because my curiosity was aroused by the reported use of the dried, roasted, and ground fruit as a coffee substitute, I tried this for myself. The flavor? Rather like a weak vegetable soup.

Location At the northern end of the park. Enter the park on Guy Park Drive. Just past the statue of Dr. Edmund A. Babler, turn right onto John Cochran Drive. Drive 1.3 miles, passing the turnoff to the left leading to the John Cochran Shelter and two turnoffs to the right leading to Babler Lodge and to the Day Use Parking Area. Park along the shoulder of the road under the electrical wires. Walk across John Cochran Drive and follow the short trail 20 yards to the Coleman-Tyler Cemetery. Turn left and walk 6 yards to find Common Horse Gentian growing along both sides of the trail. Distance: 26 yards.

Terrain From John Cochran Drive into the cemetery, the trail is 1.5–2 feet wide and of packed earth; the trail in the cemetery itself is covered with chunks of bark.

Cacalia muhlenbergii	**Great Indian**
Compositae (Asteraceae)	**Plantain**
Native perennial	Daisy family
Late May – September (June 25)	

Stem Erect, 1–3 m tall, grooved, green, and glabrous.

Flower Heads of five pale creamy to white individual tubular-shaped disk flowers occur in clusters at the top of the plant. See Botanical Terms for an explanation of the "head" of a composite flower.

Leaves Alternate; the large showy, irregularly toothed lower leaves are green on both sides, on long stems, and often wider than long. Upper leaves measure 9 cm wide by 6 cm long on stems 2 cm long.

Location Along Woodbine Trail. Enter the park on Guy Park Drive and continue for 2.1 miles. Turn right at the sign for the Nature Trail Parking Area and park in the northeast corner of the lot, near the wooden bulletin board. Walk southeast on the entrance trail for 15 yards, then right (south) on Woodbine Trail. Individual plants appear almost immediately. Then, 10 feet past the intersection with signs for Woodbine Trail and Footbridge, is the first group of Great Indian Plantain. This is 183 yards from the parking lot. Continue along the path to another group of ten to twenty plants on the left (east) side of the trail. Cross the roadway, continue south, and cross the wooden footbridge. Ten yards south of the bridge is another group. A digression to the bike path enables viewing of the plants growing along the east edge of that trail. Distance: 0.125 to 0.25 mile.

Terrain Woodbine Trail is packed earth with some gravel, 2–3 feet wide, and mostly level. The bike path is paved, 9 feet wide, and level in this area.

Seymeria macrophylla
(Dasistoma macrophylla)
Scrophulariaceae
Native perennial
June – September (July 27)

Mullein Foxglove

Figwort family

Stem Erect, 1–2 m tall, and sparsely hairy.

Flower Five-part, tubular, pale yellow, 1.5–2 cm long, and without any stalk. The flower's "face" has a flattened appearance, thus encouraging us to delight in referring to it as "a flat-faced, fern-leaved False Foxglove."

Leaves Opposite; the lower leaves are 20–40 cm long and deeply cut, while the upper leaves are lanceolate, entire, and quite small, measuring only 0.6–1 cm in length.

Location At the northern end of the park along an old, unused roadway leading toward Wild Horse Creek Road. Enter the park on Guy Park Drive and turn right onto John Cochran Drive. Drive 1.1 miles and turn right to park in the Day Use Parking Area. Walk northwest, then north along the unused roadway for 220 yards to the first sighting of Mullein Foxglove on both the left and the right sides of the trail. Take the path on the left going south-southwest for a short distance to see a dense colony of the plant. Then continue back to the parking lot, or resume the original route toward Wild Horse Creek Road for scattered Mullein Foxglove. Distance: from 0.125 to 0.75 mile, depending on your choice.

Terrain Both the 12-foot-wide asphalt and small-gravel unused roadway and the 4-to-6-foot-wide crushed-rock trail are level.

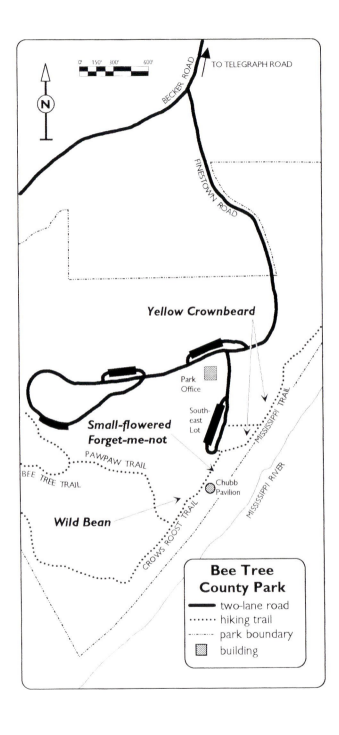

Bee Tree County Park

- two-lane road
- hiking trail
- park boundary
- building

Yellow Crownbeard

Small-flowered Forget-me-not

Wild Bean

BECKER ROAD

TO TELEGRAPH ROAD

FINESTOWN ROAD

Park Office

South-east Lot

MISSISSIPPI TRAIL

Chubb Pavilion

PAWPAW TRAIL

BEE TREE TRAIL

CROWS ROOST TRAIL

MISSISSIPPI RIVER

N

0' 150' 300' 600'

2

Bee Tree County Park

198 acres, along the Mississippi River, south St. Louis County

Entrance on Finestown Road, between Fine Road and Becker Road

Golden Eagle River Museum

St. Louis County Department of Parks and Recreation (314–889–2863)

Myosotis stricta
Boraginaceae
Introduced annual, from Europe
May–August (April 10)

Small-flowered Forget-me-not

Borage family

Seen and identified as new to the state of Missouri as recently as April 12, 1984, this delicate blue flower continued to bloom and grow for several weeks until it was mowed. Appears annually in early April.

Stem Erect, 2–20 cm tall, and covered with soft white hair.

Flower Composed of five tiny sky-blue petal-lobes around a light yellow or white center. The flowers line up on an uncoiling stem and are each 1.5–4 mm in diameter.

Leaves Oblong, 5–15 mm long and 3–4 mm wide, and covered with soft white hair.

Location On the lower half to two-thirds of the sloping lawn facing the Mississippi River near and 25 feet north of R. Walston Chubb Pavilion. Park at the southeast lot. On foot, cross the road to follow the trail toward Chubb Pavilion some 50–55 yards. Turn to face the river and look carefully. On the slope below, you will see a "carpet of blue" covering an area 32 yards long by 5 yards deep extending nearly to the pavilion. Walk down the slope for the best view. Distance: 65–70 yards.

Terrain Flat 6-foot-wide paved trail, then sloping grassy area.

Phaseolus polystachios	**Wild Bean**
var. *polystachios*	Pea (Bean) family
Leguminosae (Fabaceae)	
Native perennial	
July–September (August 9)	

Stem A vine that climbs and twists its way upward on other vegetation for 3–4 m in length.

Flower Lilac-pink, 1–1.2 cm long, with an oblique stigma. Groups of ten to fourteen flowers form racemes, with individual lower flowers opening first.

Leaves Alternate; composed of three broadly ovate leaflets, each 3–12 cm long by up to 10 cm wide and attached to the petiole. When wiping the sweat from my brow with a bandanna on a hot, humid August day, I discovered the adherent quality of the lower surface of the leaf—one had stuck itself to my bandanna.

Location Along Crows Roost Trail at the edge of the woods and 0.25 mile plus 110 yards from the south end of southeast parking lot. Most vines are on the right (west) side of the trail, but several can be found on the other side. From the parking lot, cross the road and follow Crows Roost Trail to the right past R. Walston Chubb Pavilion, then continue southwest to the first Wild Bean. Continue past the first sighting, looking carefully for additional plants in the trees and shrubs. Distance: 0.375 mile to farthest point.

Terrain Flat, 8-foot-wide blacktop surface easing into white crushed rock.

Verbesina helianthoides
Compositae (Asteraceae)
Native perennial
May–October (June 11)

Yellow Crownbeard, Wing Stem

Daisy family

Stem Erect, up to 1 m tall, and hairy, with leaf tissue extending along the stem from each leaf.

Flower Heads of yellow disk flowers and yellow ray flowers, with eight to fifteen rays on a horizontal plane, some measuring 1.8–2 cm long and 0.5–0.6 cm wide. See Botanical Terms for an explanation of the "head" of a composite flower.

Leaves Mostly alternate, entire, toothed, 6–15 cm long by 2–6 cm wide. Some leaves are lanceolate; some are closer to ovate, with the greater width toward the stem. All are roughly hairy on the upper surface and softly hairy on the underside, which is also a slightly lighter green.

Location Along the Mississippi Trail. Park halfway down the southeast lot, toward the eastern edge. Walk across the road and toward the metal bench. Follow the unmarked trail down the railroad-tie steps toward the Mississippi Trail and turn onto the packed-earth trail for a distance of 130 yards. (1) Turn left (north) onto the main trail. Within 6 feet on your left, Yellow Crownbeard appears. It continues sporadically along the trail for 110 yards. Or (2) turn right (south) and walk 125 yards farther along the Mississippi Trail for other numerous, scattered plants. Distance: 240–475 yards, depending on options chosen.

Terrain Basically flat, but the unmarked entrance trail to the Mississippi Trail is down a slope from the main body of the park. The Mississippi Trail is of packed earth and 18 inches wide.

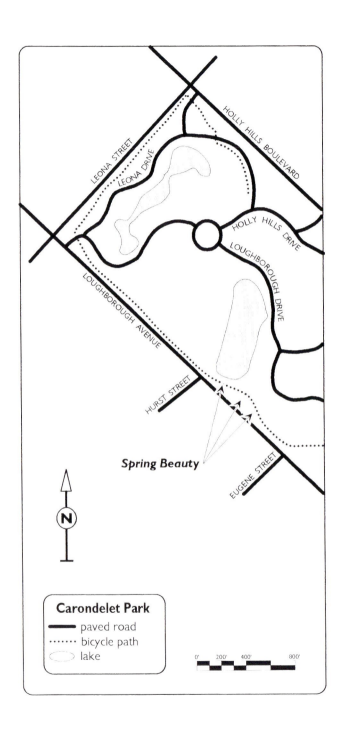

Spring Beauty

Carondelet Park

— paved road
...... bicycle path
◯ lake

N

0'   200'   400'   800'

3

Carondelet Park

180 acres, south St. Louis

Entrances from Loughborough Avenue on
the south and from Holly Hills Boulevard via
the Grand Boulevard viaduct on the north

St. Louis Department of Parks, Recreation
and Forestry, Recreation Division
(314–535–0100)

Claytonia virginica
Portulacaceae
Native perennial
February–May (March 21)

Spring Beauty

Purslane family

Stem Erect, 13–16 cm tall while the plant is in bloom.

Flower Five petals, usually white with dark pink veins, and five pink stamens. Individually stalked flowers, 1–1.5 cm in diameter, arise from an elongated common stem.

Leaves Grasslike, basal, up to 15 cm long by 1 cm wide, and arising from a small, edible (when cooked) corm. The flowering stem has only one pair of opposite leaves.

Location On the Loughborough Avenue side of the park, in the lawn between the large lake and Loughborough Avenue and primarily in the areas between Hurst and Eugene streets. Distance: variable, from 10 feet.

Terrain No trail; just walk on the lawn to observe the flowering plants.

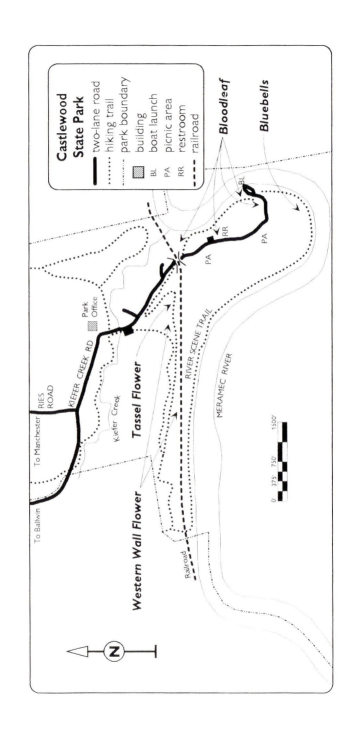

4

Castlewood State Park

1,780 acres, St. Louis County

Entrances on Kiefer Creek Road and Ries
Road, in Ballwin

Small visitor center (314–527–6481)

Missouri Department of Natural Resources

Iresine rhizomatosa
Amaranthaceae
Native perennial
August–October (August 25)

Bloodleaf

Amaranth family

Stem Erect, 0.3–1.5 m tall.

Flower Barely 0.1 cm long when fully mature, with five delicate sepals (composed of a translucent, almost sparkling tissue) and five stamens. It is the silvery white color of the bracts and calyx that make the plant quite showy in a unique way—giving it an almost ghostlike quality.

Leaves Opposite, medium green, and on petioles, which vary in length from 0.3 cm near the top of the plant to 1.5 cm near the base. The length of the blade varies from 3.5 to 12.5 cm and the width from 0.7 to 6 cm.

Location Most easily seen near the Picnic Area and restroom on the left (east) side of the road, 0.3 mile past the railroad tunnel. Park in the lot on the east side of the road and walk 50 yards northeast on the grassy area toward the edge of the woods. You are facing Bloodleaf. Follow the edge of the woods 30 yards toward the restroom for an abundant display. If you wish, continue walking along the roadside toward the Meramec River, turn left onto the paved River Scene Trail, and walk northwest along it for just over 0.25 mile for Bloodleaf scattered intermittently along the trail. At the end of the trail turn left on the main road to return to the parking lot. Distance: 0.5 mile total.

Terrain Essentially flat; River Scene Trail is blacktop and 7 feet wide.

Mertensia virginica
Boraginaceae
Native perennial
Late March–June (April 9)

Bluebells

Borage family

Stem Erect, up to 5 cm tall, and smooth.

Flower Begins as a pale pink bud but surprisingly opens into a flower with a pink or blue 2.5-cm-long tubular-shaped corolla with five shallow lobes. Up to fifteen individual flowers all on one side of the stem hang downward like bells in a cluster.

Leaves Alternate and entire; those at the base of the plant are largest, measuring up to 20 cm long, while those along the stem are considerably reduced in size.

Location In rich bottomland along the River Scene Trail close to the Meramec River. Park on the lot closest to the Boat Launch. Walk east and then south along the trail. At 0.25 mile, scattered plants appear, but best colony of approximately five hundred plants is at 0.375 mile and on the right side of the trail. Distance: 0.25 – 0.375 mile.

Terrain Packed-earth trail, sometimes quite muddy, is basically flat.

Brickellia grandiflora	**Tassel Flower**
Compositae (Asteraceae)	Daisy family
Native perennial	
July–October (September 25)	

Stem Erect, 30–90 cm tall, and minutely hairy.

Flower Cream-colored to yellowish tubular disk flowers tightly clustered into flat-topped heads, 0.7–1.4 cm in diameter. See Botanical Terms for an explanation of the "head" of a composite flower.

Leaves Mostly alternate, toothed, 3–11 cm long by 2.5–6 cm wide, and heart-shaped.

Location Along River Scene Trail, above and north of the railroad tracks. Park at the first lot on the right after crossing over Kiefer Creek. Walk southeast toward the road and very briefly along it. Turn right (south) into the woods. Follow River Scene Trail upward for nearly 0.25 mile. The main colony of eighty-five plants extends 11 feet along the trail, mostly on the left. Twenty more plants can be seen 15 feet farther along the trail. Distance: 0.25 mile.

Terrain Packed-earth trail, 18 inches wide, leads progressively upward to top of steep bluff.

Warning After leaving the low area, be careful, especially with children, as these bluffs drop off quite suddenly!

Erysimum capitatum
Cruciferae (Brassicaceae)
Native biennial
May–July (May 3)

Western Wall Flower

Mustard family

Stem Erect, 15–112 cm tall.

Flower Orange to orange yellow, 2 cm in diameter, with four rounded petals, each 0.6–1.2 cm long, arranged in an elongated raceme up to 15 cm long. Flowers on different parts of the stalk open at separate times: those at the base bloom first, those at the tip last. Fragrant and extremely attractive. We have records of these blooming here as early as April 8 and as late as June 27.

Leaves Stem leaves are alternate, narrow, 3–5 cm long by 0.4 cm wide with few rounded teeth. Basal leaves are similar in shape.

Location High up on the limestone bluffs above the railroad tracks along the River Scene Trail. Park at the first lot on the right after crossing over Kiefer Creek. Walk southeast toward the road and very briefly along it. Turn right (south) into the woods. Follow the trail upward until 0.25 mile from the parking lot; when the trail splits take the left branch and continue upward. At 0.25 mile look to the far left for plants, usually from two to nine in number; additional plants can be found at 0.375 mile, at 0.5 mile, and at 0.625 mile. We have seen as many as nineteen. Distance: from 0.25 to 0.625 mile.

Terrain Packed-earth trail 18 inches wide leading progressively upward to the top of steep bluffs.

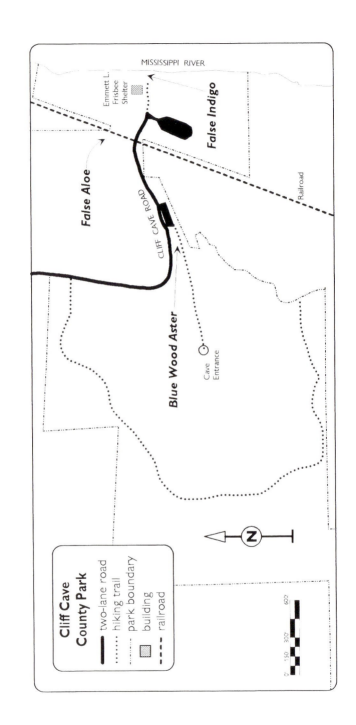

MISSISSIPPI RIVER

Emmett L.
Frisbee
Shelter

False Aloe

False Indigo

CLIFF CAVE ROAD

Railroad

Blue Wood Aster

Cave
Entrance

N

**Cliff Cave
County Park**

— two-lane road
····· hiking trail
— · — park boundary
▦ building
– – – railroad

0   150 300'   600'

5

Cliff Cave County Park

221 acres, along the Mississippi River, south
St. Louis County

Entrance from Cliff Cave Road, accessed from
Telegraph Road (Highway 231)

Designated a Natural Heritage Park in 1986
by a vote of the people of St. Louis County

St. Louis County Department of Parks and
Recreation (314–889–2863)

Aster cordifolius	**Blue Wood**
Compositae (Asteraceae)	**Aster**
Native perennial	Daisy family
August–November (September 27)	

Stem Erect, up to 70 cm tall.

Flower Pale blue heads with ten to twenty ray flowers each 0.5–1 cm long encircling a central portion composed of pale, cream-colored disk flowers, thus forming a daisylike whole 1.5–2 cm in diameter. See Botanical Terms for an explanation of the "head" of a composite flower.

Leaves Alternate, heart-shaped, sharply toothed, 3.5–12 cm long by 2.5–7 cm wide, and on long, slightly winged petioles.

Location Along the south side of Cliff Cave Road. Park in the first lot on the south (right) side of the entrance road. Walk southwest on the mowed grass for 45 yards to the concrete slab remains of a springhouse. Plants are here as well as 20 yards farther along the mowed edge and extending for 35 more yards. Distance: 45–100 yards.

Terrain Flat and grassy.

Agave virginica
(Manfreda virginica)
Amaryllidaceae
Native perennial
Late June–August (July 3)

False Aloe
Amaryllis family

Stem Erect, 1–2 m tall.

Flower A flowering spike bears greenish white tubular flowers, each 2–3 cm long and 0.3 cm wide, with stamens extending 1 cm past the fused petals and sepals. The petal and sepal tube is twice as long as the six lobes. Flowers are pleasantly fragrant.

Leaves Basal leaves, 10–20 cm long by 1–2 cm wide, are thick and fleshy. There are no recognizable leaves along the tall, naked flowering stalk.

Location On top of a steep limestone bluff in a glade directly above the railroad tracks. Access is difficult. Park at the north end of the lot closest to the Mississippi River. Walk north on the entrance road, then northwest to cross the railroad tracks. Turn right by the wooden sign prohibiting rock climbing and follow the steep, rocky trail uphill. At the 5-foot-high rocky barrier, veer left 15 feet for easier access up to the glade. Forty-three plants are directly ahead as well as scattered to your right to the overlook. Distance to this point: 333 yards.

Terrain Trail is narrow, rocky, and definitely uphill. Wear sturdy shoes or boots.

Amorpha fruticosa
Leguminosae (Fabaceae)
Native perennial
May–June (May 10)

False Indigo

Pea (Bean) family

Stem Erect, up to 5 m tall, and branching; a shrub.

Flower Flowering racemes, up to 20 cm long, composed of erect, slender individual purple florets each composed of one upper petal folded around ten orange stamens and one style. Individual florets are 6–8 mm long.

Leaves Alternate; each composed of eleven to twenty-seven oval leaflets 2–4 cm long.

Location In the floodplain of the Mississippi River. Park at the north end of the lot closest to the river. Walk north along the entrance road and turn right on the path toward Emmett L. Frisbee Shelter and flagpole, for a total distance of 192.5 yards. False Indigo is directly ahead, between the flagpole and the river and extending north to south for 45 yards. Distance: over 200 yards.

Terrain Paved, flat roadway plus flat 6-foot-wide, white, crushed-rock-covered pathway and then mowed lawn.

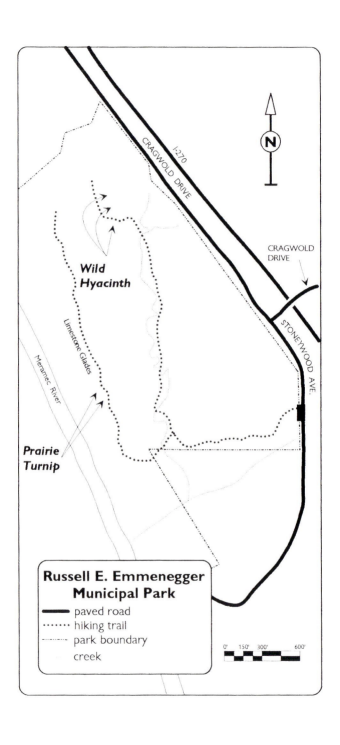

CRAGWOLD DRIVE

I-270

CRAGWOLD DRIVE

STONEWOOD AVE.

N

Wild
Hyacinth

Limestone Glades

Meramec River

Prairie
Turnip

**Russell E. Emmenegger
Municipal Park**
— paved road
···· hiking trail
–·–·– park boundary
—— creek

0'   150'   300'   600'

6

Russell E. Emmenegger Municipal Park

94 acres, St. Louis County

Entrance from Stoneywood Avenue, off
Cragwold Drive, off Geyer Road, in Kirkwood

City of Kirkwood Parks and Recreation
(314–822–5855)

Psoralea esculenta
(Pediomelum esculentum)
Leguminosae (Fabaceae)
Native perennial
Late April–July (May 8)

Prairie Turnip

Pea (Bean) family

Stem Erect, 10–30 cm tall, hairy, and branching.

Flower Purplish blue, 1.6–2 cm long, and in dense spikes; the opening of individual flowers starts at the base and moves upward.

Leaves Alternate; palmately compound with each of the five leaflets 3–4 cm long by 1 cm wide. These leaves have been seen to fold in and partially close during hot weather.

Location On limestone glades above the Meramec River. From the parking area, follow the trail into the park for 0.375 mile, then turn left (south), stepping over fallen logs and crossing the creek. The trail splits at 110 yards short of 0.5 mile. Take the trail to the right and follow it steeply uphill. At 0.5 mile turn right to go north. At 0.625 mile a glade appears on your left. Search carefully for Prairie Turnip, then continue upward to a south-facing glade on your left at nearly 0.75 mile, where ten plants can be seen. Distance: 0.625–0.75 mile.

Terrain Packed-earth trail with uneven surface is steep and rocky at times. Take care to minimize damage to the easily eroded glade areas.

Camassia scilloides	# Wild Hyacinth
Liliaceae	Lily family
Native perennial	
April–mid-May (April 18)	

Stem Erect, up to 52 cm tall, arising from an underground bulb.

Flower Delicate and fragrant, 3 cm in diameter, with three petals and three sepals of a very pale blue color and six yellow-tipped stamens. Fifteen to forty-five flowers occur on individual stalks 2 cm long arranged alternately around the central flower stalk, with total flowering area comprising up to 24.5 cm of the main stem.

Leaves Basal, folded, linear, up to 33 cm long by 0.4 – 0.8 cm wide.

Location Scattered along the main trail, going essentially north. Follow the trail and stay in the bottomland and along the creek, always choosing the trail that continues northward. Wild Hyacinth first appears at 330 yards, then near 0.25 mile off to the right. Continue north. After 0.625 mile the northbound trail goes up a slope. At 0.5 mile is the main site, mostly on your right. Total seen blooming may number 125 – 150. Distance: 0.5 mile to main site.

Terrain Primarily flat on packed-earth trail but then uphill toward the main colony. Could be slippery if wet. Several side branches can make this a confusing hike.

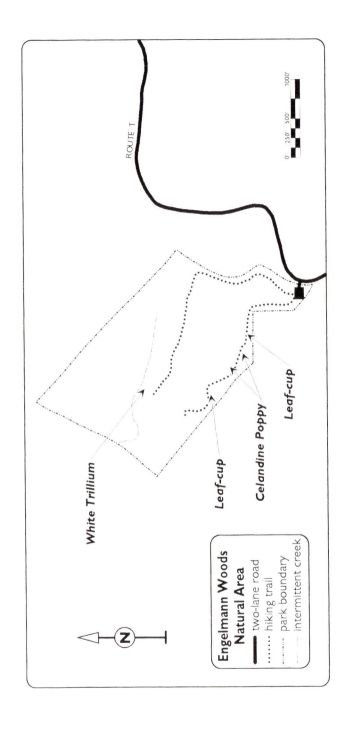

Engelmann Woods
Natural Area

two-lane road
hiking trail
park boundary
intermittent creek

N

ROUTE T

White Trillium

Leaf-cup

Celandine Poppy

Leaf-cup

0'   250'   500'   1000'

7

Engelmann Woods Natural Area

148 acres, Franklin County

Entrance on Route T is 6.1 miles west
of Manchester Road (Highway 100)
and 5 miles northeast of Labadie

Missouri Department of Conservation
(314–821–8427)

Stylophorum diphyllum
Papaveraceae
Native perennial
April–June (April 25)

Celandine Poppy

Poppy family

Stem Erect, up to 45 cm tall, and hairy.

Flower Four golden yellow petals, 1.8–3 cm long, arranged around a central cluster of one pistil and numerous stamens.

Leaves One pair of opposite, deeply lobed, and scalloped leaves on the stem plus basal leaves of similar lobing; all have a whitened lower surface and emit a poisonous yellow-orange sap when torn. The large basal leaves measure up to 25 cm long.

Location Most easily seen in the rich woods on both sides of the trail leading northwest from the parking lot. Walk north-west on the trail to the "Welcome to Engelmann Woods" sign; continue past the sign going west and then north for a total distance of 0.25 mile plus 120 yards. The first colony appears here and extends 100 yards along the trail. The next, larger colony is 70 yards farther and 25 feet off the trail to the right and left. Distance: by 0.5 mile you should have seen enough Celandine Poppy for one day.

Terrain Packed-earth trail, 1.5–2 feet wide, is uneven with exposed roots in some areas.

Polymnia canadensis	# Leaf-cup
Compositae (Asteraceae)	Daisy family
Native perennial	
May – October (August 9)	

Stem Erect, 60 –150 cm tall, branching, and glandular-sticky.

Flower Puzzling variations occur in the flower heads in that the rays may or may not be present. If present, the rays are white with three lobes and up to 10–12 mm long. Disk flowers are muted yellow and 6–13 mm in diameter. See Botanical Terms for an explanation of the "head" of a composite flower.

Leaves Large opposite leaves, up to 30 cm long, are thin-textured with toothed lobes and feel sticky to the touch. Both flowers and leaves emit a distinctive but elusive scent upon bruising.

Location Along the trail leading northwest from the parking lot. Walk northwest on the trail to the "Welcome to Engelmann Woods" sign; continue past the sign going west and then north approximately 10 yards to the first Leaf-cup on the right at 0.25 mile from the parking lot. The plant grows in scattered colonies along both sides of trail for 110 yards or more. After a brief interval without any Leaf-cup, it appears again, sometimes in the trail and sometimes up to 21 feet off the trail and down the slope to the right. Distance: 0.375 mile to farthest plants.

Terrain Packed-earth trail, 1.5–2 feet wide, is uneven with exposed roots in some areas.

Trillium flexipes
Liliaceae
Native perennial
April–May (April 25)

White Trillium
Lily family

Stem Erect, up to 60 cm tall; here usually only to 40 cm tall.

Flower Three white petals and three green sepals grow at the end of a 10-cm-long horizontally spreading (sometimes re-flexed) stalk. Each petal is up to 4 cm long by 2 cm wide; each sepal is up to 3.5 cm long by 1.7 cm wide. The peduncle can also be vertical and the flower itself flexed.

Leaves Sessile, three in number, nearly round, sometimes longer than wide (12 cm long by 11.5 cm wide) and sometimes wider than long (14.5 cm wide by 13 cm long), with sharply pointed tips.

Location In the ravine of the intermittent creek running essentially east and west. From the parking lot, go around the gate to follow an old packed-earth roadway northeast and then pick up the narrow trail marked by footprint signs. When the trail splits, follow the footprint sign to the left. At 0.9 mile, the trail ends at a wooden sign. Work your way carefully down the very steep north-facing slope on your right to the ravine for the White Trillium. A bonus plant here is the Celandine Poppy. Distance: 1.5 miles.

Terrain Easy, flat, well-maintained trail at the beginning with the route becoming exceedingly difficult and steep upon leaving the trail. Wear long pants to protect against the stinging hairs of the abundant Wood Nettle.

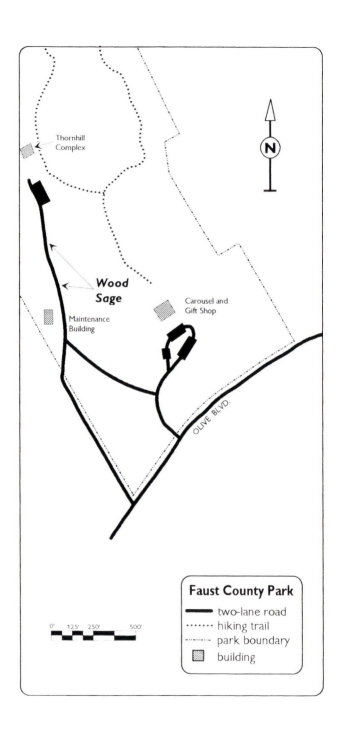

Thornhill
Complex

*Wood
Sage*

Carousel and
Gift Shop

Maintenance
Building

OLIVE BLVD.

Faust County Park

— two-lane road
····· hiking trail
—··— park boundary
▨ building

N

0'   125'   250'   500'

8

Faust County Park

98 acres, St. Louis County

15185 Olive Boulevard, in Chesterfield

Thornhill Historic Site (314–532–7298) and St. Louis Carousel (in operating condition and enclosed in a building with a small museum and gift shop) (314–537–0222)

St. Louis County Department of Parks and Recreation (314–889–2863)

Teucrium canadense	**Wood Sage**
Labiatae (Lamiaceae)	Mint family
Native perennial	
June–September (June 21)	

Stem Erect, 30–90 cm tall, square, and covered with short soft hair.

Flower Lavender pink and numerous, arranged in a terminal spike on a 0.1–0.3 cm pedicel. Each corolla has five uneven lobes each 2 cm long. We refer to the individual flowers as "topless" because the upper lobes are so small and offset as to appear absent, leaving bare the four arching stamens. Delicately scented.

Leaves Opposite, ovate-lanceolate, sharply toothed, and quite hairy on the lower surface; blades are up to 10.2 cm long by 3.5 cm broad and on petioles up to 0.7 cm long.

Location At the edge of the woods on the east side of the road leading to the Thornhill complex. Park at the lot nearest the Thornhill complex. Walk back toward the park entrance along the mowed strip and close to the woods. Wood Sage begins at 45 yards and extends two-thirds of the way to the wooden maintenance building visible on the other side of the road. Beware of the Poison Ivy. Distance: 45–210 yards.

Terrain Flat, mowed, grassy area.

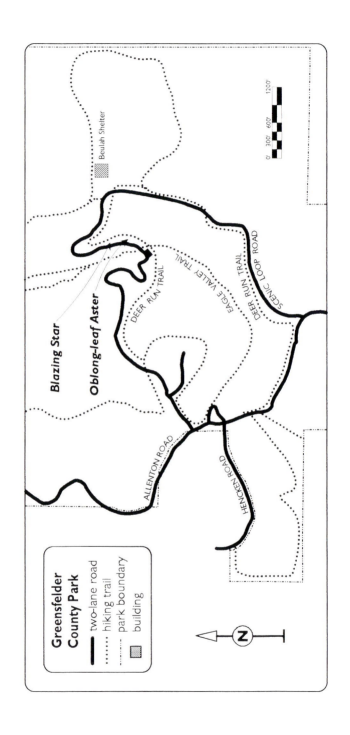

Greensfelder County Park

two-lane road
hiking trail
park boundary
building

Blazing Star
Oblong-leaf Aster

Beulah Shelter

DEER RUN TRAIL
EAGLE VALLEY TRAIL
DEER RUN TRAIL
SCENIC LOOP ROAD
ALLENTON ROAD
HENCKEN ROAD

N

0' 300' 600'   1200'

9

Greensfelder County Park

1,754 acres, St. Louis County

Allenton and Hencken Roads

Designated a Natural Heritage Park in November 1986 by a vote of the people of St. Louis County

St. Louis County Department of Parks and Recreation (314–889–2863)

Liatris cylindracea	**Blazing Star**
Compositae (Asteraceae)	Daisy family
Native perennial	
July–September (September 6)	

Stem Erect, 20–60 cm tall, glabrous, and unbranched.

Flower Rose-lavender, in flower heads arranged alternately along the spike and each composed of ten to sixty individual tubular flowers. The involucre is cylindrical with appressed, erect bracts—the plants here having rounded bracts with short tips. See Botanical Terms for an explanation of the "head" of a composite flower.

Leaves Alternate, linear, 0.2–1.2 cm wide and 10–25 cm long, with the longest leaves toward the base; smooth on the upper side and a bit rough on the underside.

Location On a limestone glade near Scenic Loop Road. Enter the park at the south entrance on Allenton Road to drive the Scenic Loop Road. Follow the road past signs to Beulah Shelter and the camera overlook, down a steep grade to the small parking area on the left where Eagle Valley Trail crosses the road. This is 1.5 miles from the park entrance. Carefully walk the road northeast (back the way you came) and uphill to the glade on your right at 220 yards. Continue walking along the road and watching the glade. Blazing Star begins at 275 yards, but the main cluster is at 0.25 mile from the parking area. Turn right and into the glade. Roam freely. Distance: 0.25 mile.

Terrain Paved road, uphill, then rocky, uneven glade.

Oblong-leaf Aster

Daisy family

Stem Erect, up to 60 cm tall, brittle, with very short stiff hair and some glands.

Flower Numerous showy heads with yellow disk flowers 1–1.5 cm in diameter surrounded by twenty-five to thirty blue-lavender ray flowers each 1–1.5 cm long. Spreading bracts have numerous stalked glands as well as hair. The scent of the crushed flower heads is somewhat akin to turpentine. The disk turns reddish brown with age. See Botanical Terms for an explanation of the "head" of a composite flower.

Leaves Upper leaves on the main stem are alternate, entire, and up to 5 cm long and 0.8 cm wide with the base somewhat clasping the stem. Longer lower leaves are often dried up at flowering. Most noticeable are the numerous, alternate, entire, quite small (5–8 mm long by 2 mm wide) leaves of the flowering branches. All leaves have a gray-green color, possibly due to the numerous hairs.

Location On a limestone glade near Scenic Loop Road. Enter the park at the south entrance on Allenton Road to drive the Scenic Loop Road. Follow the road past signs to Beulah Shelter and the camera overlook, down a steep grade to the small parking area on the left where Eagle Valley Trail crosses the road. This is 1.5 miles from the park entrance. Walk Eagle Valley Trail south for 20 feet; turn left onto the narrow, unmarked trail and go northeast until reaching glade. Several areas of Oblong-leaf Aster can be seen within 0.25 mile. Distance: 0.25 mile.

Terrain Narrow, packed-earth trail, occasionally rutted with hoofprints and slightly uphill.

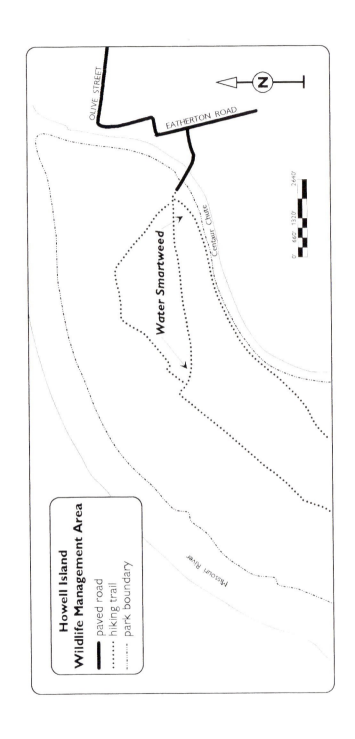

10

Howell Island Wildlife Management Area

2,547 acres, south of the Missouri River and north of Centaur Chute, St. Charles County

Entrance causeway reached from Eatherton Road

Missouri Department of Conservation

Contact for local information: Busch Wildlife Area Headquarters, St. Charles (314 – 441 – 4554)

Polygonum coccineum
(Polygonum amphibium
var. *emersum)*
Polygonaceae
Native perennial
June – October (September 11)

Water Smartweed

Buckwheat family

Stem A variable plant with swollen nodes, having terrestrial and aquatic forms, but those in our area are usually standing erect in or near water and 60–90 cm tall.

Flower Flowering raceme, 4–15 cm long and 1 cm thick, is composed of numerous individual flowers with no petals, only five sepals of a very deep pink hue with pale pink stamens, and pistils extending 1.5 times the length of the sepals. Each flower has a dark maroon center.

Leaves Simple, alternate, ovate-lanceolate, up to 20 cm long, and tapering to the tip. Note the papery sheaths along the stem at the leaf bases.

Location Along the trail going west. Drive over Centaur Chute causeway to park on Howell Island near the orange metal gate. Walk under or around the gate to follow the trail, heading northwest and then west for a total of 120 yards. Water Smartweed is primarily on the left (south) side of the trail and extends for 100 yards with some interruptions. The next main colony is at 1.625 mile and on the right. Distance: 120 yards–1.625 mile.

Terrain Flat, wide roadway of packed earth and mowed vegetation; can be quite muddy at times.

Note Ragweed has for the most part finished blooming by this time, but mosquitoes can be a terrible bother.

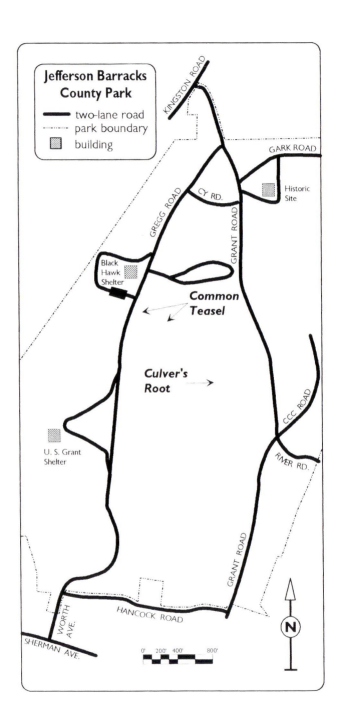

11

Jefferson Barracks County Park

425 acres, partly along Mississippi River, south St. Louis County

Entrances from Sherman and Worth Avenues on the south and Broadway/Kingston Road on the north

Jefferson Barracks Historic Site (314–544–5714)

St. Louis County Department of Parks and Recreation (314–889–2863)

Dipsacus sylvestris
(Dipsacus fullonum)
Dipsacaceae
Introduced biennial or perennial,
from Europe
June – October (July 15)

Common Teasel

Teasel family

Stem Erect, up to 180 cm tall, sturdy, and prickly.

Flower Oval flower heads to 7 cm long appear lilac in color due to densely packed individual tubular, white florets 1–1.5 cm long with 0.1 cm long lavender lobes. Spinelike bracts extend from between the individual flowers. Additional bracts 5 – 8 cm long extend upward from the base of the flower head; some exceed the length of the flower head.

Leaves Opposite leaves on the upper stem are entire and 23 cm long by only 4 – 5 cm wide, with the wider section just above the halfway point, but tapering; each is joined at the base to the leaf opposite. The lower surface has thornlike prickles on the midvein. Basal leaves are up to 30 cm long and widest at midleaf or above and are toothed in a scalloped manner.

Location Along the edge of the woods in the northwest area of the park. Park in the southeast corner of the south lot of Black Hawk Shelter. Walk east across Gregg Road. Follow the edge of the woods to the right (south) to a wide mowed path; at the junction are the Teasel. This is 100 yards from the parking lot. Turn east to walk the wide path; Common Teasel appears at intervals (interspersed with Poison Ivy), from 50 yards up the path to 105 yards. Approximately forty-two plants are in this area. Distance: 205 yards.

Terrain Mowed, flat grassy area.

Veronicastrum virginicum
Scrophulariaceae
Native perennial
June–September (July 7)

Culver's Root

Figwort family

Stem Erect, up to 130 cm tall, brownish red, and hairy.

Flower Slender terminal spikes up to 18 cm long are composed of individual white tubular flowers measuring 0.7–0.9 cm with stamens extending above the corolla lobes.

Leaves Toothed, lanceolate, on petioles 0.3–1 cm long, and in whorls of three to six (our plants have whorls of four or five). Lower leaves are 8 cm long by 2.5 cm wide, dark green on the upper surface, and gray green and pubescent on the under surface.

Location Near the middle of the park along the edge of the woods. Park in the southeast corner of the south lot of Black Hawk Shelter. Walk south on the sidewalk along Gregg Road for 340 yards to the third upright, concrete-filled, 3-foot-high post, just before the sign and turnoff for the U. S. Grant Shelter. Turn east, cross Gregg Road, and continue east across the open field for nearly 0.25 mile to the edge of the woods. Eighteen to twenty Culver's Root plants should be directly in front of you. Distance: nearly 0.5 mile.

Terrain Flat concrete sidewalk and nearly flat, mowed, open field.

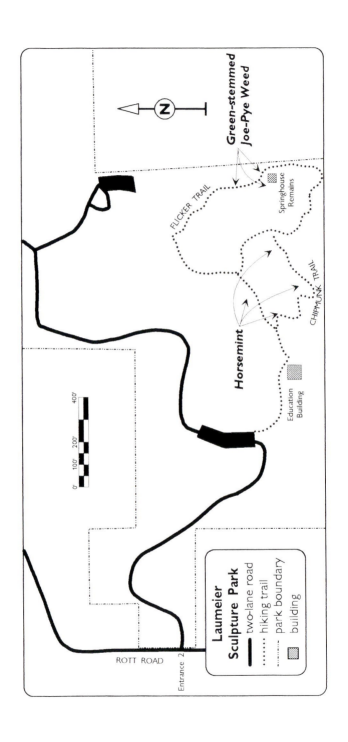

Green-stemmed Joe-Pye Weed

FLICKER TRAIL

Springhouse Remains

Horsemint

CHIPMUNK TRAIL

Education Building

N

0' 100' 200' 40'

Laumeier Sculpture Park

——— two-lane road
·········· hiking trail
—··—··— park boundary
▨ building

ROTT ROAD

Entrance 2

12

Laumeier Sculpture Park

96 acres, St. Louis County

12580 Rott Road, with two entrances from
Rott Road at Geyer Road, in Sunset Hills

Orientation Center and Gallery Gift Shop
(314–821–1209)

St. Louis County Department of Parks and
Recreation (314–889–2863)

Eupatorium purpureum
Compositae (Asteraceae)
Native perennial
July – September (July 21)

Green-stemmed Joe-Pye Weed
Daisy family

Stem Erect, up to 180 cm tall, solid, mostly smooth, green with purple at the leaf nodes.

Flower Pink, mauve, or lilac dome-shaped heads 12 cm wide by 11 cm high are composed of numerous individual disk flowers, each 1.8 cm long, grouped together on individual stems at different levels. Buds are first green, then white or pink. Reported to have the scent of vanilla. See Botanical Terms for an explanation of the "head" of a composite flower.

Leaves In whorls of three and four; some plants have whorls of four along the entire stem, but others have whorls of four in the lower half and whorls of three in the upper half. The diameter of the whorls is widest at midstem. The larger individual leaves are 29 cm long by 11 cm wide.

Location In the southeast area of the park, along the trail leading to the old springhouse remains. Enter the park from the west at Entrance 2 and drive to the parking lot, parking at the south end. Follow the paved trail to and past the Education Building and then past the wood bench, continuing northeast on Flicker Trail. At just past 0.25 mile turn right to go essentially southeast, and soon right again. A wooden bench on the left and a packed-earth trail to the right indicate the area of Green-stemmed Joe-Pye Weed. Turn right onto this trail. From this point until you arrive at the springhouse remains, Joe-Pye Weed is abundant (104 plants one year). Distance: 0.375 mile to first sighting.

Terrain Blacktop trail, 9 feet wide, from the parking lot to the Education Building, then wood-chip or packed-earth trails, 2–3 feet wide; mostly level but sloping downward near the end.

Monarda russeliana	# Horsemint, Beebalm
(Monarda bradburiana)	Mint family
Labiatae (Lamiaceae)	
Native perennial	
Late April–June (May 10)	

Stem Erect, up to 50 cm tall, smooth, and usually unbranched.

Flower Usually one dense cluster per plant composed of irregular tubular florets, each having a short upper lip of mauve with hairs at the tip and a lower, longer, recurved lip that is a combination of pink and white, dotted with maroon spots, and ends in a small clawlike tip.

Leaves Opposite, nearly stalkless, lanceolate, up to 10 cm long and 5 cm wide, with inconspicuous teeth.

Location Toward the southern end of the park along the Chipmunk Trail. Enter the park from the west at Entrance 2 and drive to the parking lot, parking at the south end. Follow the paved trail to and past the Education Building to the first trail on your right. Turn right on this narrow, packed-earth trail, designated as Chipmunk Trail on the map. Horsemint appears on the left within 10 yards, and then again 40 yards farther, on the left and beside the second railroad-tie step. Distance: 200 – 240 yards. To see more Horsemint follow the trails to your left, circling back to the Education Building and the parking lot. Distance: 0.5 mile.

Terrain Blacktop trail, 9 feet wide, from the parking lot to the Education Building, and then packed-earth trail with railroad-tie steps.

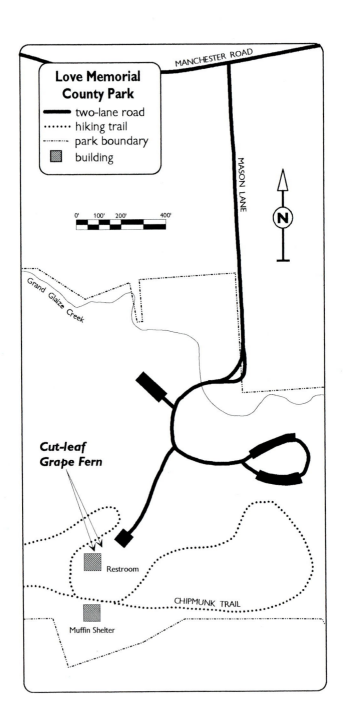

13

Love Memorial County Park

51 acres, St. Louis County

Take Mason Lane south from
Manchester Road (Highway 100)
to the park entrance

St. Louis County Department
of Parks and Recreation
(314–889–2863)

Botrychium dissectum var. *dissectum*
(Botrychium dissectum f. *dissectum)*
Ophioglossaceae
Native perennial
Mature spores August–
November (October 19)

Cut-leaf Grape Fern

Adder's-tongue family

Plant Height 41 cm. Stemless aboveground. The leaf has a petiole that splits at or near the base into a stalked, lacy blade and a highly modified fertile portion with a long stalk and a dense cluster of ball-like sporangia along the top. This is a fern, so no flowers are produced.

Sporangia Green to golden, round, and surrounding branchlike structures at the top of the fertile spike. Each sporangia is 0.1–0.2 cm in diameter. The fertile portion is 13 cm long.

Leaves Sterile blades up to 18 cm long by 15 cm wide, broadly triangular in outline, and on a stalk up to 9 cm long. The blades are lacy and finely divided into numerous leaflets and lobes that end in squared-off areas with notched tips. The leaves turn bronze during the fall and remain fresh and alive through the winter.

Location In the southwest corner of the park near Muffin Shelter. Park in the lot for Muffin Shelter. Walk west to the edge of the woods, then southwest toward the restroom, looking to your right. Three types of *Botrychium,* including the Cut-leaf Grape Fern, can be seen here. Distance: 8–15 yards.

Terrain No trail, just level, mowed area to the edge of the woods.

Note Obviously, this is not a wildflower, so why is it included? I like it! And I am always excited to have it appear on wildflower walks, so I thought you should be aware of it as well.

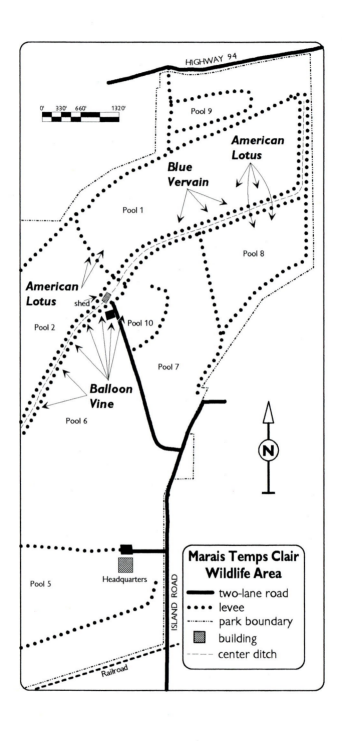

14

Marais Temps Clair Wildlife Area

918 acres, St. Charles County

Two entrances from Island Road (which heads north from Route H); one entrance from Highway 94

No visitor center but a small headquarters building

Missouri Department of Conservation

Contact for local information: Busch Wildlife Area Headquarters, St. Charles (314–441–4554)

The disastrous summer flood of 1993 resulted in damage to the levees. Subsequent maps may show different pool number designations. Telephone for current information.

Nelumbo lutea	**American Lotus**
Nymphaeaceae (Nelumbonaceae)	
Native perennial	Water Lily family
Late June–September (July 18)	(Lotus family)

Stem Not visible as it creeps along the bottom of the pool.

Flower Solitary, 15–25 cm in diameter, rising above the water on a stalk up to 120 cm in length, and composed of as many as twenty-one combined petals/sepals, each up to 12.5 cm long by 6.5 cm wide. The inner petals are creamy yellow and a third longer than the creamy green outer sepals. A circle of stamens surrounds a golden core, which is shaped like the pouring section of an old-fashioned sprinkling can. This serves as a receptacle for the ten to twelve hard, round seeds. The dried fruits are often used in crafts.

Leaves On long petioles that attach to the blades at the middle. Individual, circular blades are up to 41.5 cm in diameter, water-repellent, and blue-green. Some leaves float on the water surface, but others rise above it.

Location The closest location is on either side of the levee road separating Pool 1 from Pool 2. After turning onto Island Road, pass the gravel road to the Headquarters and continue to the next gravel road on the left. Turn left and drive to the parking lot at the northeast corner of Pool 6. Walk toward the shed, turn right (northeast), and walk past two fenced-in Restricted Areas on the left. Continue past one more Restricted Area sign. At 300 yards, on both the right and the left, is the American Lotus. If you wish to see another area, head toward the levee road between Pool 1 and Pool 8. Distance: 300 yards to the first location.

Terrain Flat, 8-foot-wide crushed-rock levee road.

Note I suggest that you wear a wide-brimmed sunhat, as this area has little shade.

Cardiospermum halicacabum
Sapindaceae
Introduced annual, from tropical America
July–September
(flower, August 15) (ripe fruit, October 3)

Balloon Vine

Soapberry family

Stem Erect, then climbing by tendrils attached to various nearby plants; this interesting vine grows to more than 2 m in length.

Flower Small and white, 5 mm in diameter, with four petals and four sepals, two of which are larger than the other two. Upon close inspection with a magnifying lens, four upright petal-like appendages can be seen toward the center of the flower; two of these have a bright yellow band at the upper edge. Flowers and fruits appear nearly continually from August through mid-October.

Leaves Alternate and divided two or three times, with individual leaflets ovate and deeply toothed; up to 15 cm long with the blade itself up to 9 cm long by 13 cm wide. Each leaf appears to be opposite a flowering stalk with tendrils. Occasionally, alternating leaves are so close that they appear to be opposite.

Fruit A three-part capsule, up to 3 cm in diameter, containing smooth, round black seeds with a white heart-shaped pattern along one side. When quite fresh, this fruit resembles an inflated balloon, thus the common name. The exterior color turns from green to warm peach to rusty brown.

Location Possibly along the center ditch of every levee road in the area. Plants can be seen easily by parking in the lot at the northeast corner of Pool 6 and walking west, then southwest on the levee road. Search carefully as the other vegetation is tall and can obscure the delicate Balloon Vine. Distance: by 0.25 mile, twenty-five to thirty plants can be seen.

Terrain Flat, 8-foot-wide, crushed-rock levee road.

Verbena hastata	# Blue Vervain
Verbenaceae	Vervain family
Native perennial	
June – October (August 21)	

Stem Erect, up to 80 cm tall, square, and roughly hairy.

Flower Lilac, five-lobed, and tubular. Individual flowers 0.2 cm across are arranged in dense terminal spikes up to 12 cm long.

Leaves Opposite, petioled, sharply saw-toothed, varied in shape, and up to 15 cm long. Most upper leaves are individual, some middle leaves have two smaller leaves at their base, and most lower leaves have basal lobes pointing outward at an angle of 40 – 45 degrees, thus the species name "hastata."

Location On the bank of the center ditch between Pool 1 and Pool 8. Park in the lot at the northeast corner of Pool 6. Walk toward the shed, turn right (northeast), and walk past two fenced-in Restricted Areas on the left. Turn right on the first road and walk northeast, then east past a red metal gate and along the canal on the south side of Pool 1. At 0.5 mile, look to the far left, some 8 feet away from the levee road and toward the center ditch. Continue to search the margins of the center ditch for more plants. Distance: 0.5 mile.

Terrain Flat, 8-foot-wide crushed-rock levee road plus downward sloping vegetative area toward center ditch.

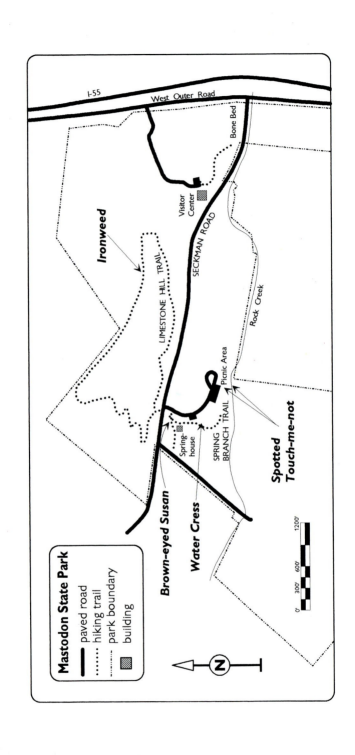

15

Mastodon State Park

425 acres, Jefferson County

1551 Seckman Road, Imperial; from
Kimmswick exit of Interstate 55, follow
signs to the park entrances: one off West
Outer Road, and one off Seckman Road

Visitor center (314–464–2976)

Missouri Department of Natural Resources

Rudbeckia triloba
Composite (Asteraceae)
Native biennial or
short-lived perennial
June – November (July 28)

Brown-eyed Susan

Daisy family

Stem Erect, up to nearly 3 m tall, very hairy, with many flowering branches.

Flower Heads composed of dark purple-brown tubular disk flowers in dense clusters 0.8–1.5 cm across, surrounded by eight to twelve deep yellow-orange rays, each 1–3 cm long. We most often see them with eight rays. See Botanical Terms for an explanation of the "head" of a composite flower.

Leaves Middle stem leaves are either trilobed or entire on a petiole 4 cm long, with the blade measuring 10 cm long by 2.5 cm wide. Lower stem leaves are trilobed and toothed on a petiole 3.5 – 4 cm long, with the blade measuring 12–14 cm long by 8 cm wide. The middle lobe of the lower leaves is also lobed. The lower leaves are often dried up and difficult to distinguish during the blooming period.

Fruit The crushed, dried seedhead emits a turpentine-like scent.

Location In a low section of the park off Seckman Road. Enter the park from Seckman Road and park at the first lot on the right. From the northwest corner of the lot, follow the access trail 35 yards to Spring Branch Trail. Turn right (north) and pass the stone springhouse on the left. The trail branches at 100 yards. Brown-eyed Susan is at this fork and along the trail heading both to the left and to the right. Turn right and follow the trail nearly parallel to Seckman Road to a mowed area. Turn right to return to the parking lot. Distance: 270 yards.

Terrain Flat, narrow, packed-earth trail, 2 feet wide narrowing to 1 foot in width.

Vernonia baldwinii | **Ironweed**
Compositae (Asteraceae) | Daisy family
Native perennial
Late May–September (July 15)

Stem Erect, up to 180 cm tall, and softly hairy.

Flower Heads approximately 8 mm wide on stalks of various lengths have thirteen to thirty-four purple, tubular, lobed, densely packed disk flowers each, but no ray flowers. Involucral upright bracts with recurved tips are resinous toward the tip along the prominent midrib. When the plant is in seed, the bracts open to a horizontal alignment for easier seed dispersal. See Botanical Terms for an explanation of the "head" of a composite flower.

Leaves Alternate, finely toothed, dark green, pointed at the tip, and measuring up to 15 cm long by 6 cm wide, with the widest area at or below the middle of the leaf.

Location In an open area at the top of a hill along the Limestone Hill Trail. Enter the park from Seckman Road and park at the first lot on the right. Walk back to Seckman Road and cross it to begin the Limestone Hill Trail. Take the trail to the right (east) for 0.75 mile plus 110 yards. Utility lines overhead indicate that you are in the right spot to see Ironweed on the left and right for 100 yards. Distance: 0.75 miles plus 180 yards.

Terrain Packed-earth trail sloping steadily upward, then leveling out as you approach the site.

Impatiens capensis	# Spotted Touch-me-not
Balsaminaceae	
Native annual	Touch-me-not
Late May–October (August 16)	family

Stem Erect, up to 180 cm tall.

Flower Orange with maroon spots and lines on the five petals (which appear as three) and mostly solid in color on the sac and spur formed by sepals; 2.5 to 3 cm long. Note that the spur often recurves to become parallel with the underside of the sac.

Leaves Alternate, simple, toothed, and up to 4.5 cm long by 2.5 cm wide. The juice of the crushed leaf is believed useful for relieving the irritation caused by poison ivy and insect bites.

Fruit A capsule, 1.5–2 cm long, that when ripe and touched by man or beast splits into five coils that disperse the seeds explosively.

Location On both banks as well as a gravel bar of Rock Creek, south of the picnic area. Enter the park from Seckman Road and park at the second lot on the right. From the southeast corner of the lot, walk south through the picnic area to Rock Creek and down the slope onto the gravel bar. When utility lines are directly overhead, Spotted Touch-me-not is to the left as well as across the creek. Distance: 150 yards.

Terrain Flat and grassy through the picnic area, then sloping slightly onto the gravel bar of Rock Creek.

Note Waterproof boots would be appropriate for the gravel bar.

Nasturtium officinale
(Rorippa nasturtium-aquaticum)
Cruciferae (Brassicaceae)
Introduced perennial, from Eurasia
April–October (May 21)

Water Cress

Mustard family

Stem Erect, then creeping or floating to nearly 100 cm tall and up to 2 cm in diameter; frequently seen with numerous slender white roots at nodes.

Flower A green center surrounded by four white, rounded petals each 4 mm wide. Individual flowers are gathered in terminal clusters.

Leaves Alternate, up to 11 cm long, dark green, and glabrous. Each leaf is divided into three to nine opposite and separate leaflets of various sizes but all with wavy margins; five leaflets have been most commonly noted.

Location In the small creek flowing from Bollefer Spring. Enter the park from Seckman Road and park in the first lot on the right. From the northwest corner of the lot follow the signs for Spring Branch Trail first west and then south to the wooden bridge. Water Cress will be visible immediately. Distance: 40 yards.

Terrain Flat, packed-earth trail.

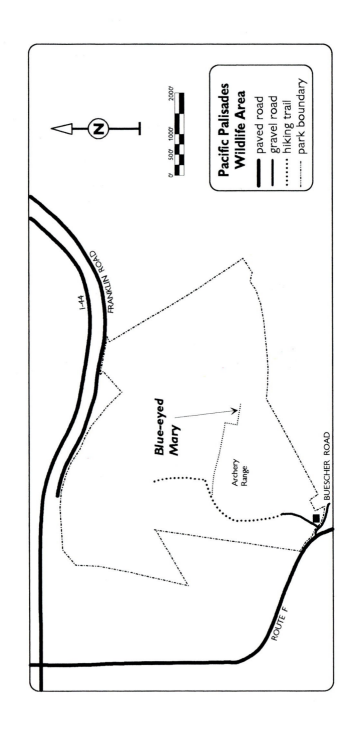

Pacific Palisades Wildlife Area

— paved road
— gravel road
· · · · · hiking trail
–·–·–· park boundary

N

0' 500' 1000' 2000'

I-44

FRANKLIN ROAD

Blue-eyed Mary

Archery Range

BUESCHER ROAD

ROUTE F

16

Pacific Palisades Wildlife Area

692 acres, St. Louis and
Jefferson Counties

Entrance road from Buescher
Road, off Route F, 0.1 mile
southeast of Pacific

Missouri Department of
Conservation (314–821–8427)

Collinsia verna	**Blue-eyed Mary**
Scrophulariaceae	Figwort family
Native annual	
April–June (April 13)	

Stem Erect, up to 35 cm tall, but weak and often leaning over near the base; somewhat hairy toward the base.

Flower Tubular, 1–1.2 cm long, and bicolored, with two white upper lobes, two blue or rose lower lobes, and a fifth lobe folded up vertically between the two lower lobes. Each of the upper and lower lobes has a small notch.

Leaves Opposite, egg-shaped, and somewhat toothed. Leaves on middle and upper stem are sessile, clasping, 4 cm long, and up to 2 cm wide. The lowest leaves are on short stalks, while those directly below the flowering area are sometimes whorled.

Location In rich bottomland beginning at 0.875 mile from the parking lot. Walk on the roadway heading essentially north and past the sign designating the fenced Archery Range on the right. At just under 0.5 mile turn right (east) to follow the Archery Range fence. Continue due east along the edge of the cultivated field until 0.75 mile from the parking lot, then turn right (south) into the woods for another 75 yards to reach a trail. Turn left (east) on the trail. At a total distance of 0.875 mile, Blue-eyed Mary begins to cover the ground. By 1 mile, you should have seen up to a thousand plants in bloom. Distance: 0.875–1 mile.

Terrain Flat, gravel road and then usually wet, muddy areas both leading to and along the narrow, flat, packed-earth trail.

Note Rubber boots are recommended for this trip.

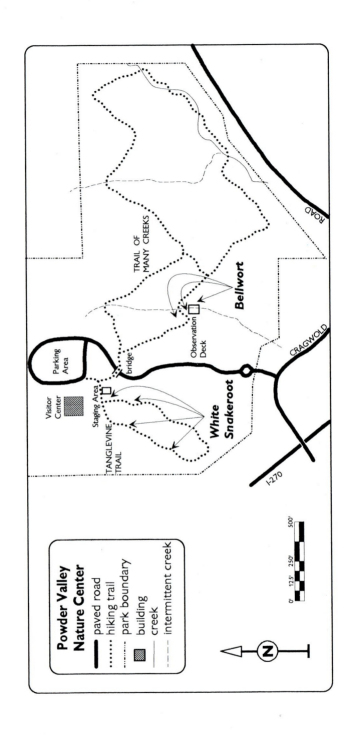

Powder Valley Nature Center

- paved road
- hiking trail
- park boundary
- building
- creek
- intermittent creek

Visitor Center

Parking Area

bridge

Staging Area

TANGLEVINE TRAIL

White Snakeroot

Observation Deck

Bellwort

TRAIL OF MANY CREEKS

ROAD

CRAGWOLD

I-270

N

0' 125' 250' 500'

17

Powder Valley
Nature Center

112 acres, St. Louis County

11715 Cragwold Road, off Geyer
Road, in Kirkwood, near intersection of Interstates 270 and 44

Visitor center

Missouri Department of
Conservation (314–821–8427)

Uvularia grandiflora	**Bellwort,**
Liliaceae	**Large Bellwort**
Native perennial	Lily family
April–May (April 13)	

Stem Erect, 20–45 cm tall during blooming period, with several sheaths hugging the lower section.

Flower Usually hangs downward, like a bell, with six lemon yellow, slightly twisted sepals/petals, separated at the base and pointed at the tip, each 7–10 mm long by 4–6 mm wide.

Leaves Alternate, sessile, up to 12 cm long, finely downy on the underside, elongated with a pointed tip, and with basal lobes meeting to surround the stem; not always open fully during flowering.

Location Along both Trail of Many Creeks and Broken Ridge Trail, but most easily located near the Observation Deck on Trail of Many Creeks. Park at the south end of the parking lot, walk south-southwest to the trail entrance, and follow the trail over the long bridge above the entrance road. When the trail splits turn right. At 170 yards from the parking lot, Bellwort appears sporadically. Continue to the Observation Deck, where Bellwort grows around all sides and across the creek as well. Continue to the wooden bridge for more plants. Distance: 0.125 mile.

Terrain Asphalt trail, nearly 6 feet wide, is mostly downhill to the Observation Deck.

Eupatorium rugosum
Compositae (Asteraceae)
Native perennial
Late July–October (September 15)

White Snakeroot

Daisy family

Stem Erect, up to 125 cm tall, and mostly smooth below the flowering part.

Flower Starkly white and tubular in clusters of twelve to twenty-four per head. Multiple terminal heads form a loose, nearly flat surface. Outer flowers reportedly open first, showing stamens rising above the other parts of the tubular disk flowers. There are no ray flowers. See Botanical Terms for an explanation of the "head" of a composite flower.

Leaves Opposite and paired, petioled, and sharply saw-toothed, with blades up to 11 cm long by 7 cm wide, broadest toward the base but tapering to a sharply pointed tip.

Location Along both sides of Tanglevine Trail. Park at the south end of the parking lot and walk south-southwest to the staging area and around to the west side of the staging area for the first major group of White Snakeroot. Walk Tanglevine Trail from the staging area, noting the abundance of these flowers at approximately 60 feet from the beginning of this loop trail. Complete the full loop of the trail for scattered occurrences. Distance: 0.3 to 0.5 mile.

Terrain Flat asphalt trail, nearly 6 feet wide, is wheelchair accessible.

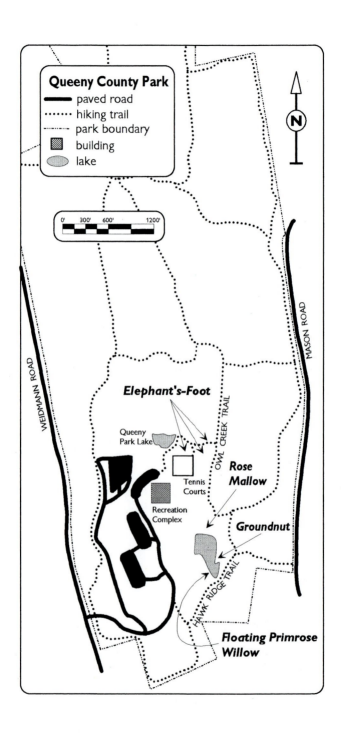

18

Queeny County Park

569 acres, St. Louis County

550 Weidmann Road, Ballwin, entrances
from Weidmann Road and Mason Road

Designated a Natural Heritage Park in
November 1986 by a vote of the people of
St. Louis County

Greensfelder Recreation Complex
(314–391–0900)

St. Louis County Department of Parks
and Recreation (314–889–2863)

Elephantopus carolinianus
Compositae (Asteraceae)
Native perennial
August–October (September 12)

Elephant's-Foot

Daisy family

Stem Erect, up to 110 cm tall, very hairy on lower half, and much branched.

Flower Lilac, pink, or white and arranged in a terminal cluster of individual flowers. Each individual tubular flower has five petal-like lobes fanned out in a semicircle. When four of these tubular flowers bloom at the same time with all the lobes outward, they look like one flower. At times, as many as sixteen tubular flowers bloom simultaneously. All of these are disk flowers. The total grouping is set off by a distinctive arrangement of three ovate bracts (2 cm long) immediately below the flowering heads. Watch for this flower to open fully in the afternoon. See Botanical Terms for an explanation of the "head" of a composite flower.

Leaves Alternate, simple, toothed, hairy, narrowing abruptly toward the base and into a winged petiole, and up to 20 cm long by 10 cm wide, the basal leaves being the largest.

Location Along the trail north of the tennis courts. Enter the park from Weidmann Road. From the parking lot behind (north of) the Greensfelder Recreation Complex, walk the roadway/trail going northeast toward Queeny Park Lake. Turn right at the lake to follow the trail around the east side of the lake and then southeast. At 120 yards, on your right, are six to seven plants. Continue southeast and downhill. Main colonies of Elephant's-Foot begin just past the paved trail leading south to the tennis courts and continue intermittently to the wooden bridge at 285 yards. Distance: 120–285 yards.

Terrain Trail is 6–7 feet wide, paved, and slightly downhill toward the wooden bridge.

Jussiaea repens var. *glabrescens*
(Ludwigia peploides)
Onagraceae
Native perennial
May – October (August 12)

Floating Primrose Willow

Evening Primrose
family

Stem Horizontal, either floating on the water or creeping along the muddy shore and rooting from the nodes; spongy, white projections seen at intervals along the stem are air roots.

Flower Five yellow petals, each 1.2 cm wide by 1.8 cm long on stalks to 7 cm long. These petals fall off easily.

Leaves Alternate, entire, oblong to spoon-shaped, on petioles up to 3 cm long, and with blades up to 6 cm long by 2 cm wide.

Location At the south end of the park. Enter the park from Weidmann Road and drive just over 0.2 mile to park along the shoulder of the entrance road near the bulletin board and Hawk Ridge Trail. Walk the paved trail (which also serves as a roadway for park vehicles) southeast and then left and north past the covered 1982 bridge. At 330 yards from the car, a lake can be seen to your left. Floating Primrose Willow grows in the water at the shoreline, as near as 10 yards to the trail. Distance: 340 yards.

Terrain Wide, flat, paved roadway-trail and then flat, grassy area.

Apios americana
Leguminosae (Fabaceae)
Native perennial
June – September (August 18)

Groundnut

Pea (Bean) family

Stem A vine, sprawling and twining and climbing up other vegetation for support; up to 3 m long.

Flower Muted in color with a dusty rose exterior and velvety maroon interior, 1–1.3 cm in length, and irregular in shape with five petals: an upright "standard," two "wings" along the side, and two lower petals fused into a boat-shaped "keel." Groups of individual flowers arise from the leaf axils in densely packed racemes, those lowest on the stalk blooming first.

Leaves Alternate, compound, 11–18 cm long, and each composed of five to seven leaflets, each of which is 4– 6 cm long by 2–3.5 cm wide, broadest toward the base, and pointed at the tip.

Location At the south end of park near the lake. Enter the park from Weidmann Road and drive just over 0.2 mile to park along the shoulder of the entrance road near the bulletin board and Hawk Ridge Trail. Walk the paved trail southeast and then left and north past the covered 1982 bridge. At 330 yards from the car, a lake can be seen to the left. Continue to the east side of the lake, then digress north from the trail to the memorial tree and bench. Walk 15–20 feet farther northwest to an "island" of trees and shrubs. Groundnut twines and climbs up these trees and shrubs on all sides. Distance: under 0.25 mile.

Terrain Wide, flat, paved trail, then flat, grassy area.

Note Groundnut grows exceedingly well in my front yard, establishing precedence over all else unless controlled. One method of control is to eat them. The cooked tuberous, thickened areas of the underground stems taste like a rather dry Irish potato. I boiled several, then sliced and fried others. If you want to try this, grow your own supply.

Hibiscus lasiocarpos
Malvaceae
Native perennial
July–October (July 23)

Rose Mallow

Mallow family

Stem Erect, up to 2 m tall, with a few hairs.

Flower White, pale pink, or hot pink, five-petaled, and 10 – 20 cm in diameter, with each petal measuring 7–10 cm long by up to 4 cm wide. Add a crimson center and a long, sturdy stamen column, and you have a wildflower bound to make an impression at eye-level.

Leaves Alternate, triangular-ovate or ovate, with blades up to 16 cm long by 12.5 cm wide and petioles 9 cm long; softly hairy on both the upper and the lower surfaces, but much more so on the lower.

Location In southeast section of the park, just north of the large lake and south of Owl Creek Trail. Enter the park from Weidmann Road and drive just over 0.2 mile to park along the shoulder of the entrance road near the bulletin board and Hawk Ridge Trail. Walk the paved trail southeast and then left and north past the covered 1982 bridge, past the lake, and past a culvert, until you are in line with the north end of the lake. Cut left (west) across the grass to the north end of the lake and turn to face north, away from the lake. Rose Mallow is growing in the wet area 12–15 feet distant. Distance: approximately 0.375 mile.

Terrain Hawk Ridge Trail is 6–7 feet wide, paved, and flat. The rest of the route is flat, grassy, and possibly slippery with duck and goose droppings.

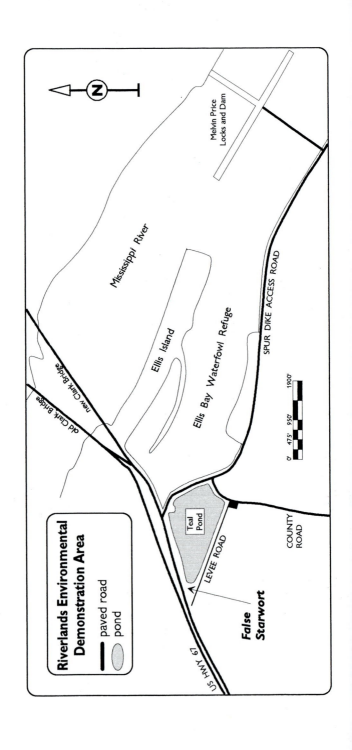

19

Riverlands Environmental Demonstration Area

1,200 acres (800, native prairie; 300, shallow marsh; 100, firebreaks and others), St. Charles County

Entrance from Highway 367/67 east onto Spur Dike Access Road, in West Alton

Visitor orientation facility

U.S. Army Corps of Engineers, St. Louis District (314–889–0405)

Boltonia asteroides var. *decurrens*
(Boltonia decurrens)
Compositae (Asteraceae)
Native short-lived perennial
July–October (September 7)

False Starwort, Decurrent False Aster

Daisy family

Stem Erect, up to 165 cm tall.

Flower In heads up to 1.3 cm in diameter. Ray flowers are white with a lavender tint and become more lavender with age; disk flowers are yellow and compressed into a dome shape. See Botanical Terms for an explanation of the "head" of a composite flower.

Leaves Alternate, entire, blue green, with leaf tissue extending down the stem from the base of the leaf to form a narrow "wing." The lower stem has ridges where earlier "wings" have dried up and disappeared. Young plants 30–75 cm tall have been noticed to have grass-green leaves.

Location Near Teal Pond. Park in the lot for Teal Pond. Walk westward along the top of the levee past Teal Pond and toward Highway 67 for 0.5 mile minus 110 yards. Turn right and descend the grassy slope, climbing over chunky rocks to reach the flat area. False Starwort begins here and extends toward the highway. Wander in the area. By 0.875 mile, you should have seen numerous plants in bloom. Distance: 0.5–0.875 mile.

Terrain Flat roadway on top of levee, 8 feet wide, with cinder and broken-rock surface, then uneven climb over large rocks to low, possibly wet area.

Note The disastrous summer flood of 1993 may have affected the location of these plants. Check at the office for current information.

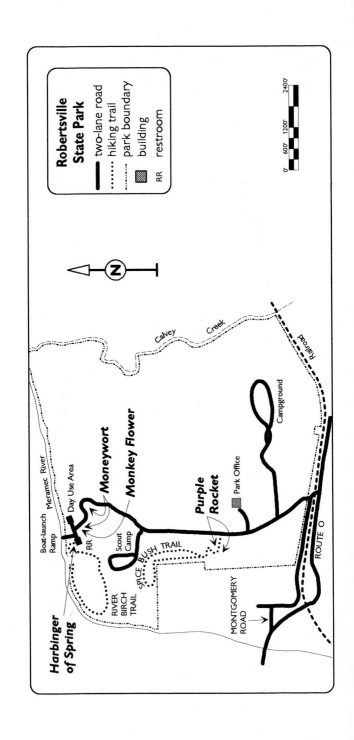

Robertsville State Park

— two-lane road
⋯ hiking trail
– – – park boundary
▨ building
RR restroom

0' 600' 1200' 2400'

N

Calvey Creek

Railroad

Meramec River

Boat-launch Ramp

Day Use Area

Harbinger of Spring

Moneywort

Monkey Flower

RR

Scout Camp

SPICE BUSH TRAIL

RIVER BIRCH TRAIL

Purple Rocket

Park Office

Campground

MONTGOMERY ROAD

ROUTE O

20

Robertsville State Park

1,109 acres, along the Meramec River,
Franklin County

From the Fire Protection District building
on the south side of Route O in Robertsville,
go west and northwest for 0.7 mile; turn
right on Montgomery Road and follow it for
only 0.1 mile; turn right again onto the state
park road, which runs parallel to railroad
tracks; another 0.7 mile will bring you to the
park entrance

Office but no visitor center

Missouri Department of Natural Resources
(314–257–3788)

Erigenia bulbosa
Umbelliferae (Apiaceae)
Native perennial
January–April (March 10)

Harbinger of Spring

Parsley (Carrot) family

Stem Erect, commonly 5 – 9 cm tall, smooth, and sometimes maroon in color.

Flower The five white petals and five maroon anthers of this delicate flower have given rise to one of its common names: Pepper and Salt. Harbinger of Spring refers to the earliness of its bloom. Even though several flowers are grouped together in an umbel, that umbel is only 5 – 7 mm in diameter.

Leaves Most plants have one leaf, which is sheathed at the junction with the flower stalk, hairless, and repeatedly divided into three parts. This results in an open, delicate structure of many small lobes.

Location In the floodplain along the Meramec River near the boat-launch ramp. Drive completely through the park to the parking lot for the restroom and boat-launch ramp. Walk 30 feet toward the river. Search carefully in the leaf litter, as most plants are only 5 – 7.5 cm tall when the flowers are at their peak. Hundreds can be found here. Head west (left) on the River Birch Trail for more Harbinger of Spring on both sides of the trail as far as 0.5 mile. Distance: 10 yards–0.5 mile.

Terrain Flat and open to the west of the boat-launch ramp, then mostly flat and sometimes muddy along the River Birch Trail.

Moneywort

Primrose family

Stem Prostate, creeping and trailing to a length of 50 cm, and smooth.

Flower Yellow, to 3 cm in diameter, each on an individual stalk arising from a leaf axil.

Leaves Opposite, grass-green, smooth, on 0.2 cm petioles, and nearly round in shape. For example, blades that are 1.8 cm long are 1.4 cm wide; the largest are 3 cm long. It is the circular shape of the leaves that reminded early botanists of coins, giving us the present-day species name *nummularia*, from the Latin *numisma* and the Greek *nomisma*, pertaining to coins.

Location In the floodplain at the north end of the park. Drive completely through the park to the parking lot for the rest-room and boat-launch ramp. Turn around in the lot, check your odometer, and drive 0.2 mile back toward the park entrance. Park briefly alongside the road. Moneywort is to your right, covering an area approximately 12 by 20 yards, but you must search carefully for the elusive flowers. Distance: 6–26 yards. Moneywort can also be seen at the Monkey Flower site.

Terrain Flat, open, grassy area.

Mimulus alatus
Scrophulariaceae
Native perennial
June–September
(August 11)

Monkey Flower, Sharp-wing Monkey Flower

Figwort family

Stem Erect, up to about 1 m tall, smooth, and slightly winged on the angles.

Flower Lilac pink, 2–2.5 cm in length, tubular, each on a stalk up to 1 cm long arising from a leaf axil. Upper lip erect with two lobes; lower lip three-lobed with two yellow spots.

Leaves Opposite, ovate, toothed, on petioles up to 2 cm long, and with blades up to 9.5 cm long.

Location In a wet ditch at the north end of the park near the Day Use Area. Drive north through the park and turn right to park in the Day Use Area. Walk south back along the entrance road to a culvert. The ditch to the right (west) has hundreds of Monkey Flower plants in it. One year 422 plants were seen in bloom. If you walk in the ditch southwest for 55 yards, you will see the main colony. Distance: 0.125 mile.

Terrain Flat road to the culvert, uneven rock and earth to descend into the ditch, and then relatively flat and possibly muddy through the ditch.

Note Wear long pants. The tall grass in the ditch will lacerate bare legs.

Iodanthus pinnatifidus
Cruciferae (Brassicaceae)
Native perennial
May–June (May 19)

Purple Rocket

Mustard family

Stem Erect, up to nearly 1 m tall, and smooth.

Flower On terminal spikes up to 18 cm long. Each flower has four white to exceedingly pale lilac petals in an *X* configuration; petals are 0.4–0.5 cm long and widest near the tip. Blooming begins closest to the leaves and continues up the spike.

Leaves Alternate, smooth, oblong to lanceolate, sharply toothed (with nearly every tooth shorter or longer than those next to it), tapering to a petiole-like section that may be slightly clasping the stem. Midstem leaves are up to 8 cm long by 2.5 cm wide; lower leaves are larger. The midrib and veins are prominent.

Location In low, wet areas along Spice Bush Trail. Drive north through the park to the parking lot on the west side of the road for the Spice Bush Trail. Walk along the trail for 165 yards to the first Purple Rocket, on your left. Continue 4 yards farther and note plants on the right. Don't turn onto the wooden bridge to your left; instead take the narrow trail straight ahead (north) to view scattered plants on both sides of the trail. Distance: by 0.375 mile you should have seen a sufficient number.

Terrain Trail is 3.5 feet wide with a wood-chip surface and primarily level with some sloping areas.

Note Be sure to use insect repellent, as mosquitoes seem to hold conventions in the area.

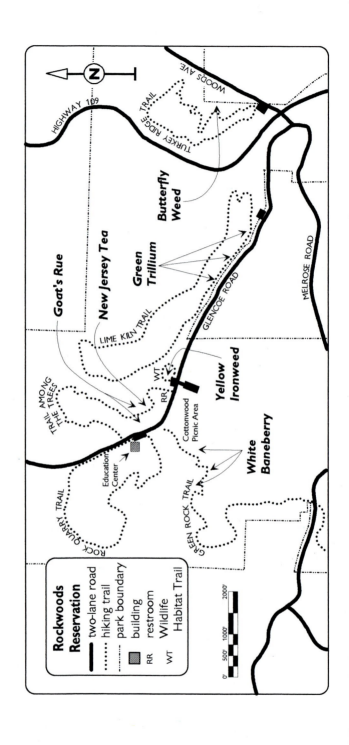

21

Rockwoods Reservation

1,898 acres, St. Louis County

Access from Highway 109 at Melrose Road in Glencoe

Education center and office (314–273–5436)

Missouri Department of Conservation, St. Louis Forest District, Regional Headquarters, Glencoe (314–458–2236)

Asclepias tuberosa
Asclepiadaceae
Native perennial
May–September (June 15)

Butterfly Weed
Milkweed family

Stem Erect, up to nearly 1 m tall, and hairy.

Flower Individual flowers, with erect orange hoods (coronas) above the reflexed orange petals and sepals, are 1.2 to 1.7 cm long and on stalks arising from one point. This creates a stunning mass of brilliant color. Flowers can be yellow, but none of this color has appeared in the colony described.

Leaves Alternate (on main stem), simple, up to 10 cm long, linear to lance-shaped, with a rounded base attached to a very short petiole, and softly hairy.

Location In the eastern part of the reservation, along the Turkey Ridge Trail. Park in the lot off Woods Avenue. Walk the trail, watching for Butterfly Weed scattered on either side beginning at 160 yards. The main colony is at 0.25 mile plus 25 yards. When the trail turns left (north), continue straight-ahead (east) to find a colony of numerous plants 8–10 yards off the trail. A wooded strip 11 feet wide separates you from yet another group of Butterfly Weed to the east. Need more? Return to the main trail and continue north for 18 yards. By looking in all of these places, it is possible to see more than a hundred flower stalks in various stages of bloom. Distance: 0.25 mile plus 120 yards.

Terrain Packed-earth trail, 3.5–4 feet wide, climbs steadily with stone steps at one point; the site of the main colony is level.

Tephrosia virginiana	**Goat's Rue,**
Leguminosae (Fabaceae)	**Hoary Pea**
Native perennial	Pea (Bean) family
May–August (June 16)	

Stem Erect, 20–50 cm tall, with soft, wavy, white or gray hair, thus the common name of Hoary Pea. The roots are known to contain rotenone (an insecticide that has proved to be poisonous to fish), so the plant is no longer fed to goats.

Flower Racemes at the top of the plant are 4–8 cm long and composed of flowers each 2 cm long with the standard (top petal) cream colored and the wings and keel pink.

Leaves Alternate and compound, with five to twenty-one individual leaflets, each oblong and up to 3 cm long; gray and softly hairy.

Location Along Trail among the Trees. Park at the restroom on the north side of Glencoe Road. Starting along the trail from its end, walk north past the posts numbered 19, 18, and 17. The Goat's Rue colony is on your right (northeast) at first, then on your left as you progress from 17 to 16. Distance to first sighting: 0.25 mile plus 95 yards.

Terrain The trail, 4 feet wide with a blacktop surface except between 19 and 18, where it is packed earth with natural rock chunks, ascends and then levels out and remains primarily level in the area of Goat's Rue.

Trillium viride
Liliaceae
Native perennial
April–May (April 17)

Green Trillium

Lily family

Stem Erect, up to 40 cm tall, and smooth.

Flower Composed of three green upright petals, up to 5.5 cm long by 1 cm wide, having a narrowed purple base and three matching sepals (sometimes totally green), up to 4.5 cm long by 1.2 cm wide, that rest horizontally atop and in between the three whorled leaves.

Leaves Three per plant are sessile, whorled, rotund with pointed tips, up to 10 cm long by 6 – 6.5 cm wide, and marked with blotches of light and dark green.

Location Along Lime Kiln Trail. Park in the designated lot along Glencoe Road. Follow the trail left (west) and parallel to Glencoe Road. Within 165 yards, Green Trillium appears intermittently on both sides of the trail but most thickly on the slopes to your right, continuing nearly to the spring outlet. Distance: from 165 yards to 0.3 mile.

Terrain Packed-earth trail, 3 feet wide, is flat for this section only.

Ceanothus americanus
Rhamnaceae
Native perennial
May–November (June 12)

New Jersey Tea
Buckthorn family

Stem Erect, up to 0.5 m tall; a shrub.

Flower Dome-shaped clusters (2–4 cm in diameter) of delicate white individual flowers (each 0.3 cm in diameter) grow at the end of long (7.5 to 13 cm) stalks. Each individual flower is composed of five white petals, shaped like ladles that curve downward, allowing the yellow pollen-laden anthers on white filaments to be readily seen.

Leaves Alternate, on petioles up to 1 cm long, and noticeably hairy on the veins of the lower surface; oval blades are up to 9 cm long by 4.5 cm wide with tapered ends and minutely toothed edges.

Location Along Trail among the Trees. Park at the restroom on the north side of Glencoe Road. Starting along the trail from its end, walk north past posts numbered 19 and 18. New Jersey Tea appears on both sides of the trail at 60 yards past 18 and continues past 17. Distance: 0.25 mile.

Terrain The trail, which is 4 feet wide with a blacktop surface except between 19 and 18, where it is packed earth with natural rock chunks, ascends and then levels out near target plants.

Actaea pachypoda	**White Baneberry,**
Ranunculaceae	**Doll's Eyes**
Native perennial	Crowfoot (Buttercup)
May–June (April 27)	family

Stem Erect, 40 – 80 cm tall, smooth, and purple, with a glaucous coating and darker purple at the nodes.

Flower Small and white, growing densely on a long-stemmed (12–19 cm) terminal raceme. The flower cluster itself is approximately 3 cm long. Spatula-shaped petals, 0.25 – 0.4 cm long by 0.1 cm wide, are shorter than the numerous white stamens.

Leaves Alternate, sharply toothed, 30.5 to 35 cm long, and two to three times compound, with individual leaflets up to 10 cm long by 3 – 6 cm wide.

Fruit It is the appearance of the fruit that suggests the common name, Doll's Eyes. When ripe, each round berry is white with a black spot. Watch for it beginning in August. Thick, bright red stalks make it easy to see.

Location Along the Green Rock Trail. From the Cottonwood Picnic Area parking lot off Glencoe Road, walk northwest toward the men's restroom. Take the trail leading west and somewhat parallel to Glencoe Road to the entrance of Green Rock Trail on your left, where the sign actually states "End of Green Rock Trail." Follow Green Rock Trail across the wooden bridge and then uphill. At 0.25 mile from the parking lot, begin looking off the trail 14 feet or so to the left. Continue northwest along the trail for 55 yards more. Look about 10 feet to the left for more Doll's Eye. Continue 8 feet farther along the trail and look 4 feet to the right. Continue 14 feet farther and look 9 feet to the left. Distance: 0.25 mile to the first location.

Terrain Grassy and/or packed-earth trail varies in width from 4 feet to 2 feet; flat, then changing to a gradual uphill climb.

Verbesina alternifolia | # Yellow Ironweed
Compositae (Asteraceae) |
Native perennial | Daisy family
Early August – October (August 29) |

Stem Erect, up to 2.5 m tall, and sometimes winged on the upper section.

Flower Heads with two to eight yellow ray flowers of varying sizes up to 3 cm long, swept back and downward from the disk; disk 1.0–1.5 cm in diameter and composed of numerous individual yellow flowers. See Botanical Terms for an explanation of the "head" of a composite flower.

Leaves Alternate on the upper part of the stem but opposite on the lower part, up to 21 cm long by 7 cm wide, and lanceolate, with finely saw-toothed edges and moderately coarse hair on both surfaces.

Location Along Wildlife Habitat Trail and many other areas of the reservation. Park at the Wildlife Habitat Trail lot (if you have a handicapped permit) on the north side of Glencoe Road, or across the road at the Cottonwood Picnic Area otherwise. Follow the self-guiding trail, beginning with 1, on your left. Between 7 and 8, Yellow Ironweed becomes evident. At 15 and from then to the end of the trail, over two hundred plants can be seen. Distance: 300 yards.

Terrain Trail is 5 feet wide, blacktop, essentially flat, and wheelchair accessible.

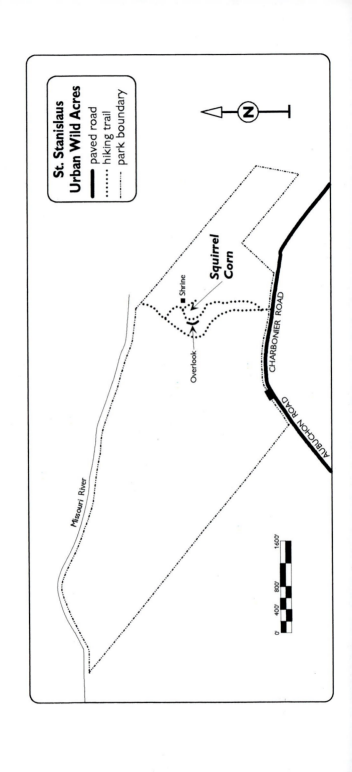

22

St. Stanislaus Urban Wild Acres

525 acres (330.62 of bottomland woods, marsh, and open land; 194.38 on Bryan Island), St. Louis County

Entrance from Aubuchon Road, which becomes Charbonier as it continues east

Missouri Department of Conservation (314–821–8427)

Dicentra canadensis	# Squirrel Corn
Fumariaceae	Fumitory family
Native perennial	
April–May (April 15)	

Stem Erect, up to 25 cm tall, and smooth.

Flower Flowering stalk comes directly from the base of the plant and rises above the leaves. Three to twelve white flowers occur on short pedicels along the stalk. Each is heart-shaped at the base, which appears to be the top since they hang reflexed. Individual flowers are heart-shaped and 2 cm long by 1.5 cm wide at the base. They are fragrant.

Leaves All basal, growing directly from a horizontal rhizome, gray green, and divided into three main parts, then finely divided and divided again. The leaves are shorter than the flowering stalks, with the largest 5.5 cm long by 6.5 cm wide.

Tubers Orange yellow in underground clusters directly at the base of the plant or horizontally 3 cm distant.

Location Near the Shrine. Park at the lot on Aubuchon Road. Walk east along Charbonier Road to the trail entrance on the left (north). Follow the trail for 165 yards and then turn on the first trail on the right (northeast). Continue north and uphill. Do not turn on the trail to the left under electrical lines but continue straight to the T junction. Turn left (northwest) to continue on the main trail along the blufftop to the overlook and the old wall at 0.875 mile from the parking lot. Continue downhill to the stone-and-chain bridge. Squirrel Corn grows in the flattened area of the small ravine and intermittently 8 feet up the west-facing slope, although it is nearly lost in the abundant Dutchman's Breeches. Distance: 0.875 mile plus 65 yards.

Terrain Charbonier Road is level and easy to walk, as is the beginning of the 8-foot-wide, packed-earth trail, but the steep climb on a 4-foot-wide packed-earth trail is difficult.

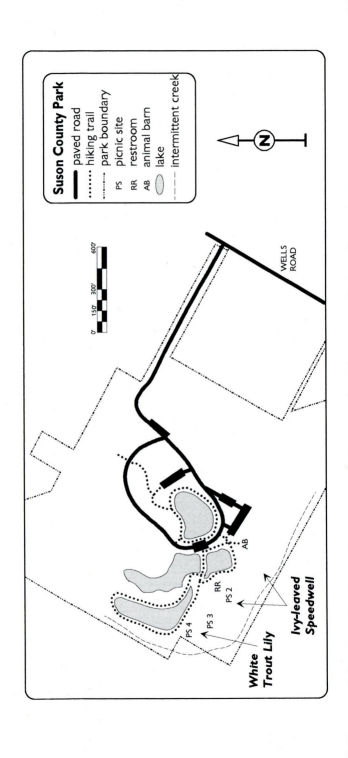

Suson County Park

— paved road
⋯⋯ hiking trail
–·–· park boundary
PS picnic site
RR restroom
AB animal barn
⬭ lake
– – – intermittent creek

N

0' 150' 300'   600'

WELLS
ROAD

AB

RR

PS 2

PS 3

PS 4

*White
Trout Lily*

*Ivy-leaved
Speedwell*

23

Suson County Park

98 acres, St. Louis County

Access from Wells Road, off Meramec
Bottom Road or Highway 21

St. Louis County Department of Parks
and Recreation (314–889–2863)

Veronica hederaefolia
Scrophulariaceae
Introduced annual, from Europe
April – May (April 9)

Ivy-leaved Speedwell

Figwort family

Stem Weak, leaning over, then sprawling along the ground, 10 – 20 cm long, hairy, and branching.

Flower Solitary, tiny (5 mm wide), blue to lilac, with four lobes, on a stalk 8–15 mm long arising from a leaf axil.

Leaves Mostly alternate, but those close to the base of the plant are opposite; the blades are hairy and nearly round in shape with three lobes (a few have five lobes) and measure 7–10 mm long by 9–12 mm wide; the stalks are up to 8 mm long.

Location Park in the lot for Suson Farm, by the Animal Barn. Walk west-northwest on the paved walkway toward the lake with the long, low, wooden bridge. Turn left to follow the gravel strip along the east edge of the lake. The Animal Barn will be to your left. Continue west-southwest, walking close to the animal-pen fence and toward the bank of the creek. Turn right to follow alongside it, searching carefully for Ivy-leaved Speedwell in both the mown and unmown areas until you are southwest of the brown restroom building. Distance: 0.125 mile plus 40 yards.

Terrain No designated trail, just the 8-foot-wide paved walkway, the 7-foot-wide gravel strip, and then level earth and grass.

Erythronium albidum var. *albidum* Liliaceae Native perennial Late March–May (April 8)	# White Trout Lily Lily family

Stem Erect, up to 30 cm tall, and coming from a single corm.

Flower Nodding, single, white, and with three petals and three sepals that are similar in appearance and each up to 3.3 cm long by 0.6 cm wide. These petals and sepals recurve as the flower matures, revealing stamens with showy, golden yellow anthers 0.8 cm long.

Leaves Apparently basal, as part of the stem is underground; oblong, 16 cm long by up to 3 cm wide, without teeth, and often blotched on both surfaces in tones of brown and green. Colonies have many more young, single-leaved plants than they do two-leaved plants bearing flowering stalks, which are usually four years or older.

Location In the west area of the park, near Picnic Site 4. Park in the designated area by the bridge over the lake and the sign for Picnic Sites 2, 3, and 4. Walk west across the bridge. Continue west past Picnic Site 3 and Picnic Site 4 toward the intermittent creek. White Trout Lily occurs mainly in the unmown area along and within 15 feet of the creek bank. Distance: 0.125 mile.

Terrain No trail, just level earth and grass areas once the bridge has been crossed.

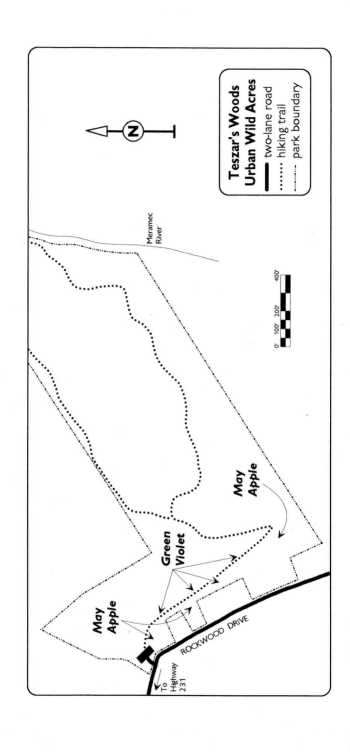

24

Teszar's Woods Urban Wild Acres

90 acres (49 in the featured tract, whose eastern boundary is the Meramec River), Jefferson County

Turn south from Telegraph Road (Highway 231) on Rockwood Drive in Arnold; go 0.3 mile to the parking lot on your left

Missouri Department of Conservation; leased to the city of Arnold

Contact for local information: Powder Valley Nature Center (314–821–8427)

Hybanthus concolor	# Green Violet
Violaceae	Violet family
Native perennial	
April–June (April 27)	

Stem Erect, up to 35 cm high, and quite hairy.

Flower Quite small, 5–7 mm in diameter, and composed of five green, notched, and recurved petals and five sepals. Each flower is on a stalk 3–5 mm long emerging from a leaf axil. This flower looks nothing like the violets with which we all are familiar.

Leaves Alternate, 8 cm long by 2.5 cm wide, broadest at the middle and tapering at the tip and base, and on petioles 1–2 cm long. The leaves present during blooming are entire and somewhat hairy.

Location Along both sides of the trail, beginning at 55–60 yards from the parking lot, densely populating slopes upward to the right and extending for 0.125 mile. Distance: 55 yards to 0.125 mile.

Terrain Packed-earth trail, 1.5 feet wide, descending gradually from the parking area to the floodplain of the Meramec River, can be quite slippery when wet.

Podophyllum peltatum
Berberidaceae
Native perennial
March–May (April 21)

May Apple, Mandrake,

Barberry family

Stem Actual stem not visible because it creeps underground. Visible "stems" are in fact leaf petioles, which are erect, up to 45 cm tall, and smooth.

Flower White, up to 5 cm in diameter, composed of from six to nine waxy petals and a very obvious greenish yellow pistil surrounded by pollen-rich stamens. Search under the umbrellalike leaves for individual flowers on nodding stems. Fragrant.

Leaves Sterile plants have only one leaf; fertile plants have two, the petioles becoming fused together about a third of the way to the ground. Radial lobing, the absence of teeth, and their large size, up to 22 cm in diameter, make these leaves memorable.

Fruit Shaped rather like an egg, 4–5 cm long, at first green in color and then ripening by July to lemon yellow. Cracking open the "shell" reveals numerous seeds with a gelatinous covering. Finding the ripe fruit is not easy as the stem with fruit on it bends toward the ground, where the fruit can be hidden in the leaves.

Location In the western area of the park, close to the parking lot and visible almost immediately along the trail and extending to a distance of 165 yards. Distance: 10–165 yards.

Terrain Packed-earth trail, 1.5 feet wide, descending gradually from the parking area to the flood plain of the Meramec River, can be quite slippery when wet.

Note All parts of the plant, except for the ripe, yellow fruit, are poisonous if ingested.

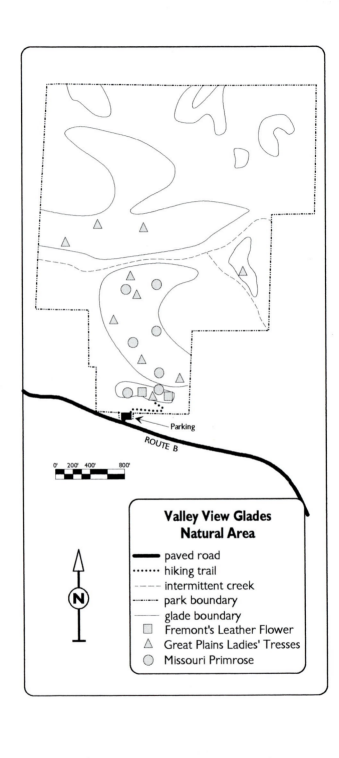

**Valley View Glades
Natural Area**

━━━ paved road
••••••• hiking trail
– – – intermittent creek
–··–··– park boundary
——— glade boundary
▢ Fremont's Leather Flower
△ Great Plains Ladies' Tresses
⬡ Missouri Primrose

Parking

ROUTE B

0' 200' 400' 800'

N

25

Valley View Glades Natural Area

227.21 acres, Jefferson County

Entrance from Route B, 2 miles southeast of Morse Mill

Missouri Department of Conservation, St. Louis Forest District, Regional Headquarters, Glencoe (314– 458–2236)

Clematis fremontii
Ranunculaceae
Native perennial
April–May (May 10)

Fremont's Leather Flower

Crowfoot (Buttercup) family

Stem Erect, up to 40 or 50 cm tall, softly hairy, and branching.

Flower Up to 4 cm long, bell-shaped, with a red-violet exterior and white interior, and on a hairy purple stalk up to 6.5 cm in length. No petals, only four sturdy petal-like sepals measuring 1.5 – 2.5 cm long and with recurved tips. Usually solitary and terminal on individual branches. Some plants seen have had up to six flowers.

Leaves Opposite, usually entire, oval with tapered ends, up to 9 cm long by 5 cm wide, leathery, and hairy, especially on the underside, with an obvious network of veins. By October and November the dried leaves have a silvery gray filigreed appearance.

Location Scattered over the first glade you come to by walking the trail from the parking lot. Distance: 155 yards from the Valley View sign at the trail entrance to the first sight of the open glade area, then varying distances to whichever plants you choose to view up close.

Terrain Packed-earth trail, 2–2.5 feet wide, slopes gradually downhill from the parking lot to the open, rocky glades.

Spiranthes magnicamporum
Orchidaceae
Native perennial
Mid September – November
(September 29)

Great Plains Ladies' Tresses

Orchid family

Stem Erect, up to 35 cm tall at this site and possibly to 60 cm elsewhere.

Flower Off-white to cream in color, 1 cm long, and with a lower lip with a yellow center and two spreading and upwardly reaching lateral sepals (rather like arms uplifted and ready to give a bear hug). The flowers are arranged in two or more spiraling ranks on a dense spike up to 14 cm in length for a plant 29 cm tall and longer on taller plants. A strong, sweet scent can be noted when in close proximity to the flowers.

Leaves Only basal, but never present at flowering time. If you are curious to see these broad linear leaves, which measure 14 cm long by 1.2 cm wide, look for them no later than August. The slender green leaflike extensions hugging the stem are actually overlapping bracts.

Location On several glades in the southern half of the natural area. From the parking lot, follow the trail to the first glade. Set up your own pattern of searching the glade; one year by crisscrossing the first glade laterally we found 73 plants (48 in bloom and 25 in bud) on just the first glade. Another year, 110 plants were noted. Distance: 0.625 mile.

Terrain Packed-earth trail, 2–2.5 feet wide, slopes gradually downhill from the parking lot to the open, rocky glades.

Oenothera missouriensis
(Oenothera macrocarpa)
Onagraceae
Native perennial
May−August (May 24)

Missouri Primrose

Evening Primrose family

Stem Erect or spreading and branching, low to the ground, and up to 50 cm long.

Flower Lemon yellow with four petals and an 8–10 cm diameter. Note the attractive yellow, cross-shaped stigma, the long corolla tube extending to the leaf axil, and the four slender, spotted sepals swept to one side. Each flower is at its peak bloom for only one day; as it ages, the color becomes muted orange. The four-angled ovary develops into an unusual capsule with four broad, papery wings.

Leaves Alternate, lance-shaped, entire, smooth, and quite sturdy; 0.5 to 10 cm long.

Location Scattered by the hundreds (maybe even a thousand) over the glades as far as the eye can see. From the parking lot, follow the trail to the first glade. Distance: 155 yards from the trail entrance to the glade, then varying distances to your choice of flowering plants.

Terrain Packed-earth trail, 2–2.5 feet wide, slopes gradually downhill from the parking lot to the open, rocky glades.

Note These outstanding flowers make it worthwhile to plan a late afternoon or early evening trip to see them.

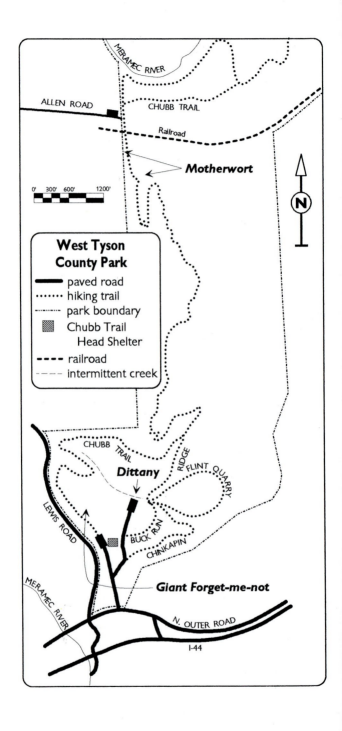

ALLEN ROAD

MERAMEC RIVER

CHUBB TRAIL

Railroad

Motherwort

N

0' 300' 600' 1200'

West Tyson County Park
— paved road
····· hiking trail
—··— park boundary
▨ Chubb Trail Head Shelter
— — railroad
— — intermittent creek

CHUBB TRAIL

Dittany

RIDGE

FLINT QUARRY

LEWIS ROAD

BUCK RUN

CHINKAPIN

Giant Forget-me-not

MERAMEC RIVER

N. OUTER ROAD

I-44

26

West Tyson County Park

663.4 acres, St. Louis County

From Lewis Road exit of Interstate 44, take
North Outer Road to the park entrance

St. Louis County Department of Parks and
Recreation (314–889–2863)

Cunila origanoides	# Dittany, Stone Mint
Labiatae (Lamiaceae)	
Native perennial	Mint family
July–November (September 13)	

Stem Erect, up to 40 cm tall, four-angled, wiry, hairy, and branching.

Flower Lavender, up to 0.8 cm long, on a short stalk, and occurring in clusters both terminal and axillary. Noticeably long stamens extend past the lip of the tubular corolla.

Leaves Opposite, roundly triangular with no petioles, finely toothed on the margin, 4 cm long by 1.5 cm wide, and glabrous. Bruised leaves emit a refreshing mint scent.

Frost flower The "frost flower" of the plant has nothing to do with the flowering part; rather it is a fluted, ribbonlike extrusion of sap and moisture from the root, which freezes as it emerges from the splitting stem near the base of the plant and can extend as far as 9 cm. Look for it in October, November, or December, when the temperature first drops below freezing.

Location On southwest- and southeast-facing slopes near the terminus of the main road through the park. Enter the park and stay on the main road to its northern end. From there walk north, down a sloping 4-foot bank to an intermittent creek. Cross the 2-foot-wide creek and walk up the gradually sloping section of the bank. (Or, scale the 6-foot-high section if you so desire!) Once across the creek, explore the southwest- and southeast-facing slopes for Dittany. Distance: only 50–55 yards from the parking lot to the first plant.

Terrain No trail, just forested slopes and the intermittent creek.

Cynoglossum virginianum	# Giant Forget-me-not
Boraginaceae	Borage family
Native perennial	
April–June (May 9)	

Stem Erect, up to 45 cm tall, hairy, and unbranched.

Flower Blue, 0.3–0.4 cm long, and funnel-shaped, with five rounded lobes. The flowers are on short stalks 0.3–1.2 cm long that are arranged alternately along flowering stems 26–30 cm tall.

Leaves Of two kinds, basal and stem. Basal leaves are up to 28 cm long by 10 cm wide, oblong, entire, strongly veined, and softly hairy. Stem leaves are up to 28 cm long by 7 cm wide, narrowly oblong, alternate, clasping, and softly hairy.

Location Along Chubb Trail. Follow the park road to the Chubb Trail Head Shelter parking area. Walk the trail. Single plants of Giant Forget-me-not appear on the right side of the trail at 50 yards, then at 120 yards and again at 275 yards. But the main colony of forty-five to fifty plants is at 0.5 mile and off the trail 15 yards to the right (southeast). Distance: 0.5 mile plus 15 yards.

Terrain Packed-earth trail, 2 to 3 feet wide, is uneven due to rock outcrops. Be aware that bicyclists use this trail and may appear rapidly with little warning.

Motherwort

Mint family

Stem Erect, up to 120 cm tall, four-angled, some singular but most branching into 3–5 flowering stalks.

Flower Pink and tubular, with two lips. The upper lip is horizontal to erect, pink with maroon lines on the inner surface and exceedingly white and hairy on the upper surface; the lower lip is deflexed to a near-vertical position, cream and pink with maroon spots and little or no hair. The flowers, 8–12 mm long, are clustered in the leaf axils.

Leaves Ranging in shape from lance-shaped with no or few teeth to palmate with five lobes and large coarse teeth; ranging in size from 3 to 12.5 cm in length, including the long petioles, and from 0.5 to 9.5 cm in width; hairy, especially on the lower surface.

Location At the northern end of the park, just south of the railroad tracks. Drive north on Lewis Road to Allen Road, then east on Allen Road for 1.1 miles to the parking area at the end of the road. Walk across the railroad tracks and continue south along the roadway into the park. At 115 yards and to your right some Motherwort can be seen. Continue south to the main colony on your left of approximately 160 plants. Distance: 275 yards from the railroad tracks.

Terrain Pedestrian-only roadway is level and 8 feet wide, with earth and rock surface.

Note Be careful. I squeezed a flower cluster once and something pricked my fingers. Was it the sharp teeth of the calyx?

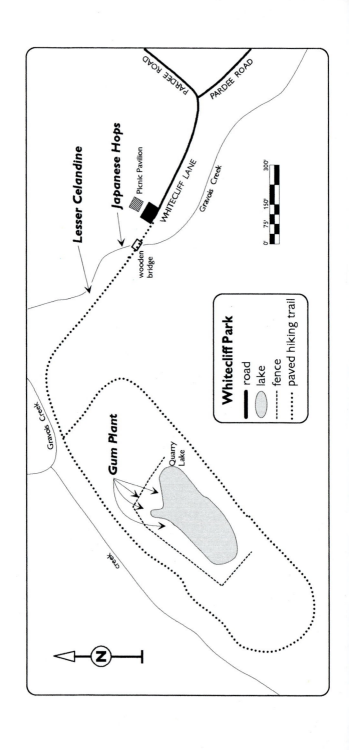

27

Whitecliff Park

80 acres, St. Louis County

9245 Whitecliff Park Lane, Crestwood;
entrance from Pardee Road to Whitecliff
Park Lane

Community Center

City of Crestwood Parks Department
(314 – 842–2122)

Grindelia lanceolata	**Gum Plant,**
Compositae (Asteraceae)	**Gumweed**
Native perennial	Daisy family
August–October (July 29)	

Stem Erect, up to 1.3 m tall, and smooth.

Flower Heads up to 3.5 cm in diameter composed of an intensely yellow disk measuring to 1.5 cm in diameter and ray flowers each up to 1.5 cm long by 0.4 cm wide. Below the flowering heads are numerous slender, spreading, green bracts that exude a sticky resin. Squeeze the involucre between your thumb and index finger to learn for yourself the origin of the common name. See Botanical Terms for an explanation of the "head" of a composite flower.

Leaves Alternate, smooth, linear to lanceolate with clasping base and saw-toothed margins (each tooth ends in a sharp bristle); up to 15 cm long by 2.5 cm wide.

Location Along the Nature Trail. As you enter the park from Pardee Road, turn right almost immediately to park in the lot by the picnic pavilion and close to the wooden bridge over Gravois Creek. Walk across the bridge and on the roadway (for use by designated vehicles only) going essentially west. Continue to the fenced-in Quarry Lake on your left. Walk toward the gate at the nearest end of the lake, where Gum Plant can be seen within several feet of the gate and fence, on both sides of it. Look to the far left inside the enclosure for the greatest abundance. Walk back to the roadway and continue past the concrete pillars and on to marker post 12. Face the lake and look inside the fence for more Gum Plant. Total plants seen should be as many as one hundred. Distance: 0.375 mile.

Terrain Flat, 10-foot-wide "roadway" with packed earth and gravel surface.

Humulus japonicus
Moraceae (Cannabaceae)
Introduced annual, from
eastern Asia
July – October (August 25)

Japanese Hops
Mulberry (Hemp) family

Stem Sprawling and creeping on the ground and climbing on other plants, up to several meters long, and sharply abrasive to the touch.

Flower On upright stems and separated as to sex. The male (staminate) flowers are the showiest with loose, graceful panicles 18–20 cm long and composed of individually stalked flowers each with five cream-to-green sepals; the female (pistillate) flowers cluster in pairs on short spikes only 10–13 cm long and on stalks up to 2.5 cm long.

Leaves Opposite; main stem leaves have five to seven lobes that are joined to the main body of the blade about two-thirds of the way toward the petiole; sharp, recurved hairs are scattered on the upper side but primarily along veins on the underside; petioles up to 27 cm long are ridged with numerous sharp, recurved hairs; blades are up to 25 cm wide with the central lobe up to 18 cm long.

Location Along the shoreline of Gravois Creek. Park in the lot by the picnic pavilion and close to the wooden bridge over Gravois Creek. Walk northwest for 40 yards to the tangled greenery and bloom of Japanese Hops. Distance: 40 yards.

Terrain No trail, just flat area of mowed grass.

Ranunculus ficaria
Ranunculaceae
Introduced perennial,
from Eurasia
April 14

Lesser Celandine

Crowfoot (Buttercup) family

Stem Reclining, but with the flowering portion erect, up to 30 cm long, smooth, succulent, and hollow.

Flower Waxy, yellow, 2–3 cm in diameter, with seven to twelve petals, and rising on an individual stalk above the leaves.

Leaves Heart-shaped with blades up to 4.5 cm long by 3.5 cm wide and petioles up to 18 cm long; margins vary from entire to wavy to bluntly toothed; underside is satiny and shiny.

Location In a low, damp area along Gravois Creek. Park in the lot by the picnic pavilion and close to the wooden bridge over Gravois Creek. Individual plants are scattered in the lawn between the parking lot and the creek. To view the large colony, walk across the bridge and along the roadway for 165–170 yards, then turn right and leave the roadway to walk 17 yards toward Gravois Creek. A Lesser Celandine colony, 45 feet by 15 feet and spreading, will be directly between you and the creek. Distance: nearly 0.125 mile.

Terrain Flat, 10-foot-wide roadway with packed earth and gravel surface.

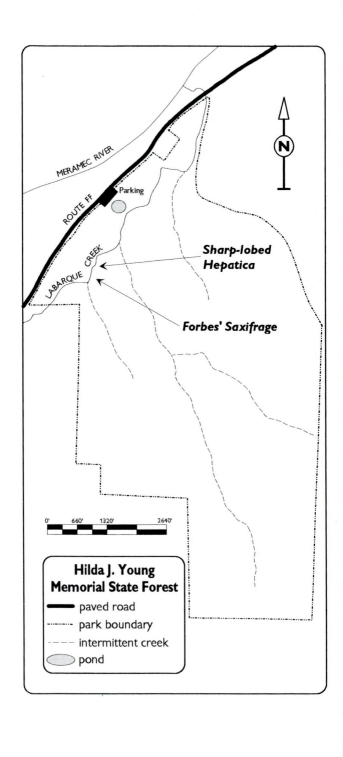

MERAMEC RIVER

ROUTE FF

Parking

LABARQUE CREEK

Sharp-lobed Hepatica

Forbes' Saxifrage

N

0'   660'   1320'   2640'

Hilda J. Young Memorial State Forest

— paved road
······ park boundary
- - - intermittent creek
⬭ pond

28

Hilda J. Young Memorial State Forest

970 acres, Jefferson County

From Eureka exit of Interstate 44, take Route W south 2.2 miles to Route FF; turn right (east) on FF and go 2.7 miles to the entrance

Missouri Department of Conservation, St. Louis Forest District, Regional Headquarters, Glencoe (314–458–2236)

Saxifraga pensylvanica
var. *forbesii*
Saxifragaceae
Native perennial
April–June (May 7)

Forbes' Saxifrage

Saxifrage family

Stem Flowering stalk up to 1 m tall; very hairy and glandular-sticky. In an "early" year, one or two plants may already be up to 25 cm tall by late March.

Flower At first, the flowering stalk has a compact cluster of buds and flowers. This extends into a stalk bearing alternately spaced flower clusters arranged loosely and openly on individual stalks of varied lengths. Individual flowers display five cream-colored petals surrounding a green center and set off by ten orange stamens; these flowers are only 6–7 mm in diameter.

Leaves Basal, dark green, oblong with a wide midrib and a tapering base, and much longer than wide, ranging from 4 to 22 cm in length and 1.5 to 9 cm in width; barely discernible toothing; hairy, with underside hair more numerous.

Location On rich, northwest-facing slopes and rock ledges 12–50 feet from LaBarque Creek. From the parking lot, walk southeast and toward the creek (away from Route FF). A pond will be to your left. At 0.125 mile plus 30 yards, turn right to go south-southwest and somewhat parallel to the creek for a total distance of 0.375 mile plus 55 yards. Cross the creek. Forbes' Saxifrage grows out of the rock faces directly ahead and to the left and right. Distance: 0.5 mile.

Terrain No designated trail, but the gradually sloping area toward the creek and the flat land parallel to the creek have usually been mowed. The creek bank and bottom can be slippery and muddy.

Note Wear calf- or knee-high rubber boots. Don't attempt to cross the creek if the water is more than 12 inches deep.

Hepatica nobilis var. *acuta*
Ranunculaceae
Native perennial
March–April (March 27)

Sharp-lobed Hepatica

Buttercup family

Stem Belowground and not visible. Apparent "stem" is actually a flower stalk, erect, up to 14 cm tall, and quite hairy.

Flower Up to 2 cm in diameter with five to twelve lilac, blue, pink, or white sepals (not petals) above three green pointed bracts. Each flower rises on its own stalk directly from the base of the plant.

Leaves All have three lobes and rise directly from the base of the plant on hairy petioles up to 14.5 cm long. In the variety growing here, the lobes taper to a point. As the flowers bloom, the leaves most noticeable are the past year's growth; these are 6–8 cm wide, have scattered hair on the underside, and are quite often maroon or bronze.

Location On rich, northwest-facing slopes and rock ledges 12–50 feet from LaBarque Creek. From the parking lot, walk southeast and toward the creek (away from Route FF). A pond will be to your left. At 0.125 mile plus 30 yards, turn right to go south-southwest and somewhat parallel to the creek for a total distance of 0.25 mile plus 60 yards. Cross the creek. Walk toward the rock ledges to the right and then south-southwest along the base and parallel to the creek for an additional 135 yards. Sharp-lobed Hepatica grows on slopes and ledges to your left. As many as 250 plants have been seen in this area. Distance: 0.5 mile.

Terrain No designated trail, but the gradually sloping area toward the creek and the flat land parallel to the creek have usually been mowed. The creek bank and bottom can be slippery and muddy.

Note Wear calf- or knee-high rubber boots. Don't attempt to cross the creek if the water is more than 12 inches deep.

Monthly Schedule

The times of peak bloom for individual wildflowers will vary widely from year to year with weather and other conditions. The dates suggested here are those that have been shown to have the best potential for attractive and abundant bloom in the specific area in which each wildflower is considered in this book. Many flowers will bloom as long as a month before or after the suggested date.

Date	Common Name	Scientific Name	Area Number
March			
10	Harbinger of Spring	*Erigenia bulbosa*	20
21	Spring Beauty	*Claytonia virginica*	3
27	Sharp-lobed Hepatica	*Hepatica nobilis* var. *acuta*	28
April			
8	White Trout Lily	*Erythronium albidum* var. *albidum*	23
9	Bluebells	*Mertensia virginica*	4
9	Ivy-leaved Speedwell	*Veronica hederaefolia*	23
10	Small-flowered Forget-me-not	*Myosotis stricta*	2
13	Blue-eyed Mary	*Collinsia verna*	16
13	Bellwort	*Uvularia grandiflora*	17
14	Lesser Celandine	*Ranunculus ficaria*	27
15	Squirrel Corn	*Dicentra canadensis*	22

Date	Common Name	Scientific Name	Area Number
17	Green Trillium	*Trillium viride*	21
18	Wild Hyacinth	*Camassia scilloides*	6
21	May Apple	*Podophyllum peltatum*	24
25	Celandine Poppy	*Stylophorum diphyllum*	7
25	White Trillium	*Trillium flexipes*	7
27	Green Violet	*Hybanthus concolor*	24
27	White Baneberry	*Actaea pachypoda*	21

May

Date	Common Name	Scientific Name	Area Number
3	Western Wall Flower	*Erysimum capitatum*	4
7	Forbes' Saxifrage	*Saxifraga pensylvanica* var. *forbesii*	28
8	Prairie Turnip	*Psoralea esculenta*	6
9	Giant Forget-me-not	*Cynoglossum virginianum*	26
10	False Indigo	*Amorpha fruticosa*	5
10	Fremont's Leather Flower	*Clematis fremontii*	25
10	Horsemint	*Monarda russeliana*	12
11	Adam-and-Eve Orchid	*Aplectrum hyemale*	1
19	Purple Rocket	*Iodanthus pinnatifidus*	20
20	Common Horse Gentian	*Triosteum perfoliatum*	1
21	Water Cress	*Nasturtium officinale*	15
24	Missouri Primrose	*Oenothera missouriensis*	25

June

Date	Common Name	Scientific Name	Area Number
8	Motherwort	*Leonurus cardiaca*	26
11	Yellow Crownbeard	*Verbesina helianthoides*	2
12	New Jersey Tea	*Ceanothus americanus*	21
15	Butterfly Weed	*Asclepias tuberosa*	21
16	Goat's Rue	*Tephrosia virginiana*	21
20	Moneywort	*Lysimachia nummularia*	20
21	Wood Sage	*Teucrium canadense*	8
25	Great Indian Plantain	*Cacalia muhlenbergii*	1

Date	Common Name	Scientific Name	Area Number

July

3	False Aloe	*Agave virginica*	5
7	Culver's Root	*Veronicastrum virginicum*	11
15	Common Teasel	*Dipsacus sylvestris*	11
15	Ironweed	*Vernonia baldwinii*	15
18	American Lotus	*Nelumbo lutea*	14
21	Green-stemmed Joe-Pye Weed	*Eupatorium purpureum*	12
23	Rose Mallow	*Hibiscus lasiocarpos*	18
27	Mullein Foxglove	*Seymeria macrophylla*	1
28	Brown-eyed Susan	*Rudbeckia triloba*	15
29	Gum Plant	*Grindelia lanceolata*	27

August

9	Leaf-cup	*Polymnia canadensis*	7
9	Wild Bean	*Phaseolus polystachios*	2
11	Monkey Flower	*Mimulus alatus*	20
12	Floating Primrose Willow	*Jussiaea repens* var. *glabrescens*	18
15	Balloon Vine	*Cardiospermum halicacabum*	14
16	Spotted Touch-me-not	*Impatiens capensis*	15
18	Groundnut	*Apios americana*	18
21	Blue Vervain	*Verbena hastata*	14
25	Bloodleaf	*Iresine rhizomatosa*	4
25	Japanese Hops	*Humulus japonicus*	27
29	Yellow Ironweed	*Verbesina alternifolia*	21

September

6	Blazing Star	*Liatris cylindracea*	9
7	False Starwort	*Boltonia asteroides* var. *decurrens*	19

Date	Common Name	Scientific Name	Area Number
11	Water Smartweed	*Polygonum coccineum*	10
12	Elephant's-Foot	*Elephantopus carolinianus*	18
13	Dittany	*Cunila origanoides*	26
15	White Snakeroot	*Eupatorium rugosum*	17
25	Tassel Flower	*Brickellia grandiflora*	4
26	Oblong-leaf Aster	*Aster oblongifolius*	9
27	Blue Wood Aster	*Aster cordifolius*	5
29	Great Plains Ladies' Tresses	*Spiranthes magnicamporum*	25

October

3	Balloon Vine (fruit)	*Cardiospermum halicacabum*	14
19	Cut-leaf Grape Fern (spores)	*Botrychium dissectum* var. *dissectum*	13

November

17	Adam-and-Eve Orchid (leaves)	*Aplectrum hyemale*	1
	Dittany	*Cunila origanoides*	26

Watch for "Frost Flower" when temperature drops to 25° for the first time

Checklist

This checklist includes many of the wildflowers that can be found at the featured areas in addition to those few highlighted in this book. The genus and species names used are primarily those found in the index of *Flora of Missouri* (1963) by Julian Steyermark. Discrepancies are due to corrections made in spelling where appropriate and to changes in the conventions for capitalization.

To determine where a specific wildflower has been found, simply locate the name in the alphabetical list, then scan the horizontal bar of the chart for marked squares. Follow the vertical bar to the top of the page for the name of the area. Additional findings can be added to the chart as desired.

Expanded information pertaining to habitat and blooming period of each plant in the checklist can be obtained from the books mentioned in References of Interest.

	Babler	Bee Tree	Carondelet	Castlewood	Cliff Cave	Emmenegger	Engelmann Woods	Faust	Greensfelder
Abutilon theophrasti			●	●					
Acalypha ostryaefolia									
Acalypha rhomboidea			●		●				
Acalypha virginica		●	●	●	●				●
Achillea millefolium	●	●		●	●		●	●	
Actaea pachypoda	●	●					●		
Agastache nepetoides	●			●	●				●
Agave virginica		●			●				
Agrimonia pubescens	●	●			●	●		●	●
Agrimonia rostellata	●	●							
Alisma plantago-aquatica									
Allium stellatum	●	●		●	●				●
Allium vineale			●	●	●	●		●	
Amaranthus tamariscinus					●				
Ambrosia artemisiifolia	●	●	●		●			●	
Ambrosia coronopifolia									
Ambrosia trifida		●	●	●	●				●
Ammannia coccinea		●	●	●					
Amorpha canescens					●				
Amorpha fruticosa					●				
Ampelopsis arborea		●							
Ampelopsis cordata				●	●			●	●
Amphicarpa bracteata	●	●		●	●		●	●	●
Amsonia illustris					●				
Anagallis arvensis		●							
Androsace occidentalis					●				
Anemone virginiana	●	●		●	●	●	●		
Anemonella thalictroides	●			●		●	●		●
Antennaria plantaginifolia	●	●		●		●	●		●
Apios americana	●	●		●					
Aplectrum hyemale	●						●	●	●
Apocynum cannabinum	●	●		●		●			
Aquilegia canadensis	●			●			●		

Howell Island

Jefferson Barracks

Laumeier

Love

Marais Temps Clair

Mastodon

Pacific Palisades

Powder Valley

Queeny

Riverlands

Robertsville

Rockwoods

St. Stanislaus

Suson

Teszar's Woods

Valley View Glades

West Tyson

Whitecliff

Hilda J. Young

	Babler	Bee Tree	Carondelet	Castlewood	Cliff Cave	Emmenegger	Engelmann Woods	Faust	Greensfelder
Arabidopsis thaliana									
Arabis canadensis									●
Arabis laevigata	●	●		●	●	●	●	●	●
Arabis lyrata									
Arabis shortii				●					
Arctium minus			●	●	●				
Arenaria patula									
Arenaria serpyllifolia	●	●		●					
Arisaema atrorubens	●	●		●	●		●		●
Arisaema dracontium	●	●		●	●	●			●
Aristolochia serpentaria	●				●				●
Aristolochia tomentosa				●					
Artemisia annua				●	●				
Aruncus dioicus		●		●	●				
Asarum canadense	●	●		●	●	●	●	●	●
Asclepias incarnata									
Asclepias purpurascens					●				
Asclepias quadrifolia	●			●			●		
Asclepias syriaca	●	●		●	●			●	
Asclepias tuberosa	●			●		●			
Asclepias verticillata				●		●			
Asclepias viridiflora						●			●
Asclepias viridis									
Aster anomalus	●	●		●	●				
Aster azureus									
Aster cordifolius				●	●			●	
Aster drummondii	●	●		●				●	●
Aster laevis									●
Aster lateriflorus	●	●		●	●			●	●
Aster linariifolius		●							●
Aster novae-angliae									
Aster oblongifolius	●	●		●					●
Aster ontarionis				●					

Checklist

Howell Island	Jefferson Barracks	Laumeier	Love	Marais Temps Clair	Mastodon	Pacific Palisades	Powder Valley	Queeny	Riverlands	Robertsville	Rockwoods	St. Stanislaus	Suson	Teszar's Woods	Valley View Glades	West Tyson	Whitecliff	Hilda J. Young
						●										●		
			●								●				●	●		
			●		●	●	●	●			●	●	●					
					●	●												
						●				●								
	●				●						●		●			●	●	
															●			
								●			●						●	
	●					●					●	●		●		●		
	●	●	●								●				●	●		
		●													●	●		
										●						●		
	●										●							
			●		●	●	●				●	●	●	●			●	
●	●		●	●				●	●			●					●	
					●													
●			●		●					●	●	●	●					●
					●	●	●				●							
											●							
						●	●	●	●	●	●				●	●		●
										●								
			●							●	●	●	●			●		
											●				●			
	●	●						●		●	●	●		●		●		●
										●								
									●									
●			●							●	●	●			●			

	Babler	Bee Tree	Carondelet	Castlewood	Cliff Cave	Emmenegger	Engelmann Woods	Faust	Greensfelder
Aster patens	●	●		●	●				●
Aster pilosus	●	●	●	●	●			●	●
Aster praealtus						●			●
Aster sagittifolius		●		●	●				●
Aster simplex		●		●					●
Aster turbinellus	●	●		●	●				●
Astragalus canadensis									
Astragalus mexicanus						●			
Atriplex patula var. hastata				●					
Baptisia australis									
Baptisia leucantha									
Baptisia leucophaea						●			
Barbarea vulgaris	●	●		●	●		●		●
Bidens aristosa									
Bidens bipinnata		●		●				●	
Bidens cernua									
Bidens comosa					●				
Bidens discoidea									
Bidens frondosa		●	●	●	●				●
Bidens polylepis				●					
Bidens vulgata				●	●			●	●
Blephilia ciliata	●			●		●		●	
Blephilia hirsuta	●			●				●	
Boehmeria cylindrica	●			●					
Boltonia asteroides var. decurrens									
Botrychium dissectum var. dissectum	●						●		
Botrychium dissectum var. obliquum	●	●					●	●	●
Botrychium virginianum	●	●					●	●	●
Brickellia grandiflora				●					
Cacalia atriplicifolia	●			●	●	●			
Cacalia muhlenbergii	●			●			●		●
Cacalia suaveolens				●					
Cacalia tuberosa						●			

Howell Island	Jefferson Barracks	Laumeier	Love	Marais Temps Clair	Mastodon	Pacific Palisades	Powder Valley	Queeny	Riverlands	Robertsville	Rockwoods	St. Stanislaus	Suson	Teszar's Woods	Valley View Glades	West Tyson	Whitecliff	Hilda J. Young
							●		●		●				●	●		
●			●			●		●	●	●	●	●	●	●	●	●	●	●
							●			●	●				●	●		
				●				●		●	●	●	●	●		●		
							●	●			●					●		
●				●														
																		●
															●			
									●									
																●		
		●	●			●		●			●		●	●		●		●
				●				●			●			●		●	●	
				●														
								●						●				
●			●	●				●		●	●					●		
●											●					●		●
		●	●	●				●	●	●						●		
								●		●	●					●		
●			●	●	●			●				●	●	●		●		
									●									
		●								●								●
		●	●					●	●	●		●	●			●		●
		●	●	●	●	●		●	●	●	●			●	●	●		●
	●	●						●		●	●			●	●	●		●
	●							●		●	●				●	●		●
						●					●				●			●
															●			

	Babler	Bee Tree	Carondelet	Castlewood	Cliff Cave	Emmenegger	Engelmann Woods	Faust	Greensfelder
Calycocarpum lyoni				●					
Camassia scilloides				●		●			
Campanula americana	●	●		●	●	●		●	●
Campsis radicans	●	●		●	●				●
Capsella bursa-pastoris		●		●	●			●	●
Cardamine bulbosa									
Cardamine parviflora var. arenicola				●			●		●
Cardiospermum halicacabum									
Carduus nutans		●		●	●	●		●	
Cassia fasciculata var. fasciculata	●	●		●	●		●		●
Cassia fasciculata var. robusta		●			●				
Cassia marilandica	●								●
Cassia nictitans				●					●
Castilleja coccinea									●
Ceanothus americanus		●		●		●			
Celastrus scandens	●	●		●				●	●
Centaurea cyanus									
Cerastium nutans							●		
Cerastium vulgatum				●				●	
Ceratophyllum demersum									
Chaenorrhinum minus				●					
Chaerophyllum procumbens	●	●		●		●	●		●
Chenopodium album		●	●	●	●				
Chenopodium ambrosioides		●	●		●				
Chenopodium gigantospermum									
Chrysanthemum leucanthemum		●			●				
Chrysopsis villosa									
Cichorium intybus		●	●	●					
Cicuta maculata									
Circaea quadrisulcata	●			●	●		●		
Cirsium altissimum	●	●		●					●
Cirsium discolor	●	●	●	●	●			●	●
Cirsium vulgare									

Howell Island	Jefferson Barracks	Laumeier	Love	Marais Temps Clair	Mastodon	Pacific Palisades	Powder Valley	Queeny	Riverlands	Robertsville	Rockwoods	St. Stanislaus	Suson	Teszar's Woods	Valley View Glades	West Tyson	Whitecliff	Hilda J. Young
																●		
					●		●				●					●		
		●	●		●		●	●		●	●	●	●	●		●	●	●
●			●		●			●	●		●						●	●
●	●	●							●		●	●				●		●
										●								
		●	●			●						●						
				●								●						
●	●							●	●			●		●				
●	●	●		●			●	●	●	●	●	●	●			●		●
				●				●						●				
●				●	●					●	●							
											●							
															●			●
												●				●		
			●		●			●			●	●					●	
										●								
	●		●			●					●		●					
				●														
		●	●		●	●				●	●	●	●	●		●		
●			●					●		●						●		
									●	●						●		
												●						
	●					●									●	●		●
															●			
														●				
										●								
												●						
																●	●	
●		●	●	●	●				●	●						●		
				●					●				●					●

	Babler	Bee Tree	Carondelet	Castlewood	Cliff Cave	Emmenegger	Engelmann Woods	Faust	Greensfelder
Claytonia virginica	●	●	●	●		●	●	●	●
Clematis dioscoreifolia									
Clematis fremontii									
Clematis pitcheri				●					
Clematis virginiana									
Collinsia verna				●		●			
Comandra richardsiana						●			
Commelina communis			●	●	●			●	●
Commelina diffusa			●	●	●				
Commelina erecta			●	●					●
Conium maculatum									
Conobea multifida									
Convolvulus arvensis		●	●			●		●	
Convolvulus sepium			●	●	●				
Corallorhiza odontorhiza				●					
Corallorhiza wisteriana	●						●		●
Coreopsis lanceolata									
Coreopsis palmata		●		●		●			
Coreopsis pubescens									
Coreopsis tripteris									●
Coronilla varia	●					●	●		
Corydalis flavula		●		●					
Croton capitatus									
Croton glandulosus				●				●	
Croton monanthogynus	●	●		●	●				●
Cryptotaenia canadensis	●	●	●	●		●	●	●	
Cunila origanoides	●	●			●	●	●		●
Cuphea petiolata									
Cuscuta species			●	●					●
Cycloloma atriplicifolium									
Cynanchum laeve			●	●					
Cynoglossum virginianum							●		
Cypripedium calceolus var. pubescens									●

Howell Island

Jefferson Barracks

Laumeier

Love

Marais Temps Clair

Mastodon

Pacific Palisades

Powder Valley

Queeny

Riverlands

Robertsville

Rockwoods

St. Stanislaus

Suson

Teszar's Woods

Valley View Glades

West Tyson

Whitecliff

Hilda J. Young

	Babler	Bee Tree	Carondelet	Castlewood	Cliff Cave	Emmenegger	Engelmann Woods	Faust	Greensfelder
Dalea alopecuroides									
Datura stramonium				●			●		
Daucus carota	●	●	●	●	●	●	●	●	
Delphinium ajacis						●			
Delphinium tricorne	●			●	●	●	●		
Dentaria laciniata	●	●		●	●	●	●		
Descurainia pinnata				●			●		●
Desmanthus illinoensis				●					●
Desmodium canescens		●							
Desmodium cuspidatum				●					●
Desmodium glutinosum	●			●	●	●	●		●
Desmodium nudiflorum				●					
Desmodium paniculatum				●	●				●
Desmodium pauciflorum									
Desmodium rotundifolium									
Dianthus armeria	●			●	●	●	●		
Dicentra canadensis				●					
Dicentra cucullaria		●		●		●	●	●	
Diodia teres	●			●					
Dioscorea batatas				●					
Dioscorea quaternata									
Dioscorea villosa	●			●	●		●		
Dipsacus sylvestris									
Dodecatheon meadia									●
Draba brachycarpa		●		●					
Draba cuneifolia				●	●				
Draba reptans				●					
Draba verna				●					
Duchesnea indica									
Echinacea pallida							●		
Echinacea purpurea									
Eclipta alba		●	●	●	●				
Elephantopus carolinianus		●			●			●	

A checklist grid with the following site columns (left to right): Howell Island, Jefferson Barracks, Laumeier, Love, Marais Temps Clair, Mastodon, Pacific Palisades, Powder Valley, Queeny, Riverlands, Robertsville, Rockwoods, St. Stanislaus, Suson, Teszar's Woods, Valley View Glades, West Tyson, Whitecliff, Hilda J. Young.

Howell Island	Jefferson Barracks	Laumeier	Love	Marais Temps Clair	Mastodon	Pacific Palisades	Powder Valley	Queeny	Riverlands	Robertsville	Rockwoods	St. Stanislaus	Suson	Teszar's Woods	Valley View Glades	West Tyson	Whitecliff	Hilda J. Young
●				●														
					●	●						●						
●	●	●	●		●	●		●	●	●	●		●	●	●		●	●
					●													
										●	●					●		
			●		●	●	●	●			●	●	●	●				●
					●													
●				●				●			●	●			●			●
					●				●		●		●					
											●					●		
		●			●	●	●	●		●	●			●		●		
								●			●					●		
●			●	●				●	●	●	●		●			●		
											●							
											●				●	●		
●	●				●	●					●		●			●		●
					●	●						●				●		
						●	●			●	●	●	●				●	●
		●																
	●	●					●			●	●			●		●		●
	●				●													
						●					●				●			●
					●		●				●					●		
					●													
																●		
					●													
			●														●	
									●	●	●				●	●		
●				●				●	●	●	●	●	●	●		●	●	●

	Babler	Bee Tree	Carondelet	Castlewood	Cliff Cave	Emmenegger	Engelmann Woods	Faust	Greensfelder
Ellisia nyctelea	●					●		●	●
Erechtites hieracifolia	●		●	●	●				●
Erigenia bulbosa							●		
Erigeron annuus	●	●	●	●	●	●	●	●	●
Erigeron canadensis		●	●	●				●	●
Erigeron philadelphicus	●	●		●		●		●	●
Erigeron pulchellus									●
Erigeron strigosus	●			●	●	●			
Eryngium yuccifolium									●
Erysimum capitatum				●					
Erysimum repandum				●					
Erythronium albidum var. albidum	●	●		●		●	●		●
Eupatorium altissimum	●	●			●	●			●
Eupatorium coelestinum				●					
Eupatorium purpureum	●	●		●				●	
Eupatorium rugosum	●	●	●	●	●			●	●
Eupatorium serotinum	●	●		●	●				●
Euphorbia commutata				●					●
Euphorbia corollata	●	●		●		●	●		●
Euphorbia dentata	●			●				●	
Euphorbia heterophylla									●
Euphorbia humistrata									
Euphorbia maculata	●	●	●	●	●	●	●	●	
Euphorbia serpens									
Euphorbia supina		●		●	●				
Fragaria virginiana				●					
Gaillardia pulchella									
Galium aparine		●		●		●	●		●
Galium circaezans	●						●		●
Galium concinnum	●	●		●					
Galium triflorum	●				●				
Gaura biennis		●		●	●				●
Gentiana puberula									

	Howell Island	Jefferson Barracks	Laumeier	Love	Marais Temps Clair	Mastodon	Pacific Palisades	Powder Valley	Queeny	Riverlands	Robertsville	Rockwoods	St. Stanislaus	Suson	Teszar's Woods	Valley View Glades	West Tyson	Whitecliff	Hilda J. Young
				●							●	●	●						
								●		●	●	●					●	●	
		●	●	●			●				●						●	●	●
	●	●	●	●		●		●	●	●	●	●	●	●	●		●	●	●
		●	●	●		●			●		●						●	●	●
			●																
			●	●		●				●	●	●						●	●
							●	●			●			●			●		
								●			●						●		
		●				●			●		●						●		
											●	●	●	●			●		●
		●		●							●		●	●	●		●		
●			●	●		●		●	●		●	●	●					●	
●		●	●	●	●	●		●	●	●	●	●	●				●	●	●
		●								●									
		●						●			●								
					●				●		●								
											●	●							
				●										●					●
				●							●				●				
●			●	●	●			●			●				●	●			
●			●								●				●				
●			●																
						●				●							●		
										●									
		●	●			●	●	●	●		●			●	●		●	●	
	●	●	●		●					●		●					●		
		●	●							●						●	●		
										●									
	●			●				●		●									●
															●				

	Babler	Bee Tree	Carondelet	Castlewood	Cliff Cave	Emmenegger	Engelmann Woods	Faust	Greensfelder
Geranium carolinianum	●			●	●		●	●	
Geranium maculatum	●	●		●		●	●		●
Gerardia flava				●					
Gerardia gattingeri									●
Gerardia grandiflora				●					●
Gerardia tenuifolia	●	●							●
Geum canadense	●	●		●	●	●		●	●
Geum vernum				●		●	●		
Gillenia stipulata	●	●		●	●	●			●
Glechoma hederacea	●		●	●	●				
Gnaphalium obtusifolium	●							●	●
Gratiola neglecta									
Grindelia lanceolata									
Hackelia virginiana									
Hedeoma pulegioides	●								
Helenium autumnale				●					
Helianthemum bicknellii									
Helianthus annuus var. annuus		●	●		●	●			
Helianthus annuus var. nanus									
Helianthus grosseserratus									●
Helianthus hirsutus	●	●		●	●				●
Helianthus maximilianii									
Helianthus strumosus		●		●	●	●	●	●	●
Helianthus tuberosus	●	●		●	●				●
Heliopsis helianthoides	●	●		●	●				●
Heliotropium indicum									
Heliotropium tenellum									
Hemerocallis fulva	●	●		●	●				
Hepatica nobilis var. acuta									
Heteranthera dubia				●					
Heterotheca latifolia				●					
Heuchera americana						●	●		
Heuchera richardsonii									

Howell Island	Jefferson Barracks	Laumeier	Love	Marais Temps Clair	Mastodon	Pacific Palisades	Powder Valley	Queeny	Riverlands	Robertsville	Rockwoods	St. Stanislaus	Suson	Teszar's Woods	Valley View Glades	West Tyson	Whitecliff	Hilda J. Young
	●			●	●		●	●	●	●	●	●		●			●	●
	●	●	●			●	●				●	●		●		●		
																	●	
															●			
											●				●	●		
								●			●							
●	●	●	●		●	●	●						●	●				
		●	●			●					●							
	●	●			●		●	●		●	●						●	
		●	●		●			●									●	
								●		●			●				●	
										●	●						●	
																		●
			●												●			
	●			●				●	●			●						●
				●				●										
				●														
								●			●					●	●	
											●							
	●	●	●		●		●	●			●			●	●			●
		●			●	●		●			●		●			●	●	
							●		●		●					●		●
														●	●			
			●		●			●		●	●	●					●	
						●												●
				●														
					●						●					●		
	●					●					●							

	Babler	Bee Tree	Carondelet	Castlewood	Cliff Cave	Emmenegger	Engelmann Woods	Faust	Greensfelder
Hibiscus lasiocarpos									
Hibiscus militaris									
Hibiscus syriacus				●					
Hibiscus trionum									
Hieracium gronovii	●			●			●		
Hieracium scabrum	●			●					●
Holosteum umbellatum		●		●					
Houstonia longifolia		●		●		●	●		●
Houstonia minima		●		●					
Houstonia nigricans				●					●
Humulus japonicus									●
Humulus lupulus	●		●	●					
Hybanthus concolor	●	●		●	●	●	●		●
Hydrangea arborescens	●	●		●	●		●		
Hydrastis canadensis	●					●	●		●
Hydrophyllum appendiculatum	●			●			●	●	●
Hydrophyllum canadense					●		●	●	
Hydrophyllum virginianum				●					
Hypericum mutilum									
Hypericum punctatum		●			●	●			
Hypericum sphaerocarpum	●			●			●		●
Hypoxis hirsuta									●
Impatiens capensis	●	●	●	●	●	●		●	
Impatiens pallida	●			●			●		
Iodanthus pinnatifidus				●					
Ipomoea hederacea									
Ipomoea lacunosa				●	●				●
Ipomoea pandurata				●	●	●			
Iresine rhizomatosa				●					
Isanthus brachiatus					●				●
Isopyrum biternatum				●			●		
Iva ciliata									
Jussiaea repens var. glabrescens			●						

Howell Island	Jefferson Barracks	Laumeier	Love	Marais Temps Clair	Mastodon	Pacific Palisades	Powder Valley	Queeny	Riverlands	Robertsville	Rockwoods	St. Stanislaus	Suson	Teszar's Woods	Valley View Glades	West Tyson	Whitecliff	Hilda J. Young
				•				•										
•												•				•		
				•					•									
											•							
												•				•		
		•											•				•	•
		•				•					•				•	•		
		•				•										•		•
														•	•			
				•												•		
			•															
			•		•		•				•			•	•			
			•		•	•					•		•	•	•			•
			•			•		•		•	•				•	•		•
						•					•							
						•												
						•												
										•			•					
		•	•		•			•					•					
													•					
															•			
		•	•	•	•	•		•				•	•					
												•				•		
						•				•								•
•		•	•		•			•	•		•							
•			•	•	•						•			•				
•		•			•			•		•	•						•	•
															•			
																•		
						•				•	•					•	•	•
•				•				•	•			•	•					•

	Babler	Bee Tree	Carondelet	Castlewood	Cliff Cave	Emmenegger	Engelmann Woods	Faust	Greensfelder
Kochia scoparia									
Krigia biflora				●			●		●
Krigia dandelion									
Kuhnia eupatorioides		●		●	●				●
Lactuca canadensis				●			●		
Lactuca floridana	●	●		●	●				●
Lactuca saligna				●					
Lactuca scariola							●		
Lamium amplexicaule		●		●		●	●	●	
Lamium purpureum				●		●		●	
Laportea canadensis	●			●		●	●		●
Lathyrus latifolius		●		●					
Lathyrus palustris									
Leonurus cardiaca									
Lepidium campestre				●					
Lepidium virginicum				●	●				
Lespedeza hirta									
Lespedeza violacea									
Liatris aspera									●
Liatrus cylindracea				●					●
Lindernia anagallidea									
Lindernia dubia				●					
Lippia lanceolata			●	●	●				
Lithospermum arvense				●					
Lithospermum canescens				●		●			●
Lobelia inflata	●	●		●	●		●		●
Lobelia siphilitica	●			●	●			●	●
Lobelia spicata									
Ludwigia palustris									
Ludwigia polycarpa									
Lycium halimifolium									
Lycopus americanus									
Lycopus virginicus			●		●				

Howell Island	Jefferson Barracks	Laumeier	Love	Marais Temps Clair	Mastodon	Pacific Palisades	Powder Valley	Queeny	Riverlands	Robertsville	Rockwoods	St. Stanislaus	Suson	Teszar's Woods	Valley View Glades	West Tyson	Whitecliff	Hilda J. Young
	●															●		
		●									●					●		
											●							
								●			●					●		
								●										
		●	●															
				●														
●			●	●	●			●	●				●					●
		●			●	●						●	●	●		●	●	●
	●	●	●			●		●			●		●			●	●	
		●	●		●												●	
				●												●		
				●	●			●										
						●					●						●	●
											●							
	●										●							
											●					●		
●					●				●	●			●					
				●				●										
●			●	●	●			●	●	●		●	●			●		●
						●	●				●	●				●		
		●	●		●			●	●	●	●		●	●		●		●
					●			●	●	●	●					●		●
											●				●			
														●				
														●				
											●							
			●	●				●										
				●				●										

	Babler	Bee Tree	Carondelet	Castlewood	Cliff Cave	Emmenegger	Engelmann Woods	Faust	Greensfelder
Lysimachia lanceolata				●					
Lysimachia nummularia			●	●					
Lythrum alatum									
Marrubium vulgare									
Matelea decipiens									●
Matricaria chamomilla				●				●	
Medicago lupulina			●	●	●				
Melilotus albus	●		●	●		●	●		
Melilotus officinalis	●		●	●	●	●		●	
Menispermum canadense	●			●		●	●		●
Mentha arvensis				●					
Mentzelia oligosperma				●					
Mertensia virginica		●		●				●	
Mimulus alatus				●					
Mimulus ringens									
Mirabilis albida									●
Mirabilis nyctaginea				●					
Mollugo verticillata				●	●				
Monarda fistulosa									●
Monarda russeliana	●	●		●		●	●		●
Monotropa uniflora				●					
Myosotis stricta		●							
Myosotis virginica		●					●		
Myosurus minimus				●			●		
Nasturtium officinale									
Nelumbo lutea									
Nepeta cataria									
Nothoscordum bivalve				●		●			●
Oenothera biennis		●	●	●	●		●		
Oenothera missouriensis									
Onosmodium occidentale						●			
Opuntia compressa					●				●
Ornithogalum umbellatum				●	●				

Howell Island	Jefferson Barracks	Laumeier	Love	Marais Temps Clair	Mastodon	Pacific Palisades	Powder Valley	Queeny	Riverlands	Robertsville	Rockwoods	St. Stanislaus	Suson	Teszar's Woods	Valley View Glades	West Tyson	Whitecliff	Hilda J. Young
										•	•				•			
			•		•	•		•		•						•	•	•
				•				•										
•																		
				•							•				•	•		
			•	•														
			•						•		•							
•	•							•		•	•		•					
•	•	•	•			•		•		•	•		•	•	•			
		•	•		•		•			•	•	•				•	•	•
				•														
			•			•	•			•								
•			•					•		•		•				•		•
•				•														
•																		
•					•				•				•	•		•	•	
	•										•							
	•	•			•		•	•	•		•			•	•	•		
											•					•		
								•										
						•						•						
									•									
					•						•							
									•									
									•									
		•		•		•					•					•		•
	•	•	•	•				•	•	•		•	•					•
															•			
				•	•						•		•			•		•
	•		•													•	•	

	Babler	Bee Tree	Carondelet	Castlewood	Cliff Cave	Emmenegger	Engelmann Woods	Faust	Greensfelder
Orobanche uniflora				●					
Osmorhiza claytonii	●			●	●	●			●
Osmorhiza longistylis	●		●			●	●	●	
Oxalis stricta	●	●		●	●		●	●	●
Oxalis violacea		●		●			●		●
Panax quinquefolium				●			●		●
Parietaria pensylvanica					●				
Parthenium hispidum						●			
Parthenium integrifolium	●			●			●		
Parthenocissus quinquefolia	●	●	●	●	●	●	●		●
Passiflora incarnata									
Passiflora lutea	●	●		●	●		●		
Penstemon digitalis						●			
Penstemon pallidus	●			●		●	●		●
Penthorum sedoides	●							●	
Perilla frutescens		●		●	●			●	
Petalostemon candidum				●					
Petalostemon purpureum						●			●
Phacelia purshii	●					●	●		
Phaseolus polystachios		●				●			
Phlox divaricata var. laphamii	●	●				●	●	●	●
Phlox paniculata		●		●	●				
Phlox pilosa		●				●			●
Phryma leptostachya	●			●	●		●	●	
Phyllanthus caroliniensis				●					
Physalis heterophylla				●	●				
Physalis virginiana									
Physostegia virginiana									
Phytolacca americana	●		●	●	●		●	●	
Pilea pumila	●	●		●	●	●	●		●
Plantago aristata	●		●		●				
Plantago lanceolata		●	●	●	●			●	
Plantago rugelii		●	●	●	●		●	●	

Howell Island	Jefferson Barracks	Laumeier	Love	Marais Temps Clair	Mastodon	Pacific Palisades	Powder Valley	Queeny	Riverlands	Robertsville	Rockwoods	St. Stanislaus	Suson	Teszar's Woods	Valley View Glades	West Tyson	Whitecliff	Hilda J. Young
											●							
		●	●								●							●
			●								●					●		
●	●	●	●	●	●	●	●	●	●	●	●	●	●		●	●	●	●
		●									●			●				
								●										
		●	●		●					●	●	●		●	●	●		●
	●				●									●				
					●			●		●	●				●			
		●	●		●	●		●			●				●			
●				●	●			●		●	●			●				●
			●		●	●	●	●		●	●	●	●				●	
								●			●							
											●							
								●			●							
		●	●				●	●			●							
													●	●				
					●						●					●		●
		●	●		●		●	●			●	●	●	●			●	
								●			●							
●																		
●																		
●								●										
												●						
●		●	●	●	●		●	●		●	●					●	●	●
●			●		●		●	●			●	●	●			●		●
		●	●	●				●	●	●	●		●	●			●	
●	●	●	●					●			●			●		●	●	●

Checklist   231

	Babler	Bee Tree	Carondelet	Castlewood	Cliff Cave	Emmenegger	Engelmann Woods	Faust	Greensfelder
Podophyllum peltatum	●	●		●	●	●	●		●
Polanisia dodecandra				●					
Polemonium reptans					●		●		
Polygonatum canaliculatum		●		●	●	●	●		
Polygonum aviculare		●	●	●	●				
Polygonum cespitosum var. longisetum	●	●	●	●	●			●	●
Polygonum coccineum						●			
Polygonum convolvulus				●					
Polygonum hydropiper						●			
Polygonum hydropiperoides									
Polygonum lapathifolium				●	●	●			
Polygonum orientale				●					
Polygonum pensylvanicum				●	●	●			
Polygonum persicaria		●							●
Polygonum punctatum				●	●				●
Polygonum scandens		●		●	●			●	●
Polygonum virginianum	●	●	●	●	●	●	●	●	●
Polymnia canadensis		●		●			●		
Polymnia uvedalia		●							
Polytaenia nuttallii	●				●				
Portulaca oleracea			●						
Potentilla norvegica				●					
Potentilla recta	●	●			●			●	
Potentilla simplex	●			●		●			●
Prenanthes altissima var. cinnamomea	●	●		●	●				●
Prunella vulgaris	●	●		●	●			●	●
Psoralea esculenta						●			
Psoralea onobrychis						●			
Psoralea psoralioides						●			
Psoralea tenuiflora									
Pycnanthemum pilosum					●				
Pycnanthemum tenuifolium		●			●				
Pycnanthemum virginianum									

Howell Island	Jefferson Barracks	Laumeier	Love	Marais Temps Clair	Mastodon	Pacific Palisades	Powder Valley	Queeny	Riverlands	Robertsville	Rockwoods	St. Stanislaus	Suson	Teszar's Woods	Valley View Glades	West Tyson	Whitecliff	Hilda J. Young
	●	●	●		●	●	●	●		●	●	●	●			●	●	
	●	●	●							●	●					●		●
			●					●			●	●			●		●	●
			●		●		●	●				●				●		
●				●					●									
●				●	●					●		●				●		
●				●			●			●		●						
●				●				●	●							●		
●		●		●	●			●	●			●		●		●		●
●		●		●				●			●	●	●				●	●
●			●	●				●		●	●	●	●				●	●
		●	●	●	●		●	●		●	●	●	●			●	●	
															●			
●				●	●											●	●	
●					●	●		●			●				●	●	●	
		●	●					●			●					●		●
		●	●				●	●						●		●		
	●	●	●		●		●				●		●	●	●			
															●			
															●			
	●				●						●				●		●	

	Babler	Bee Tree	Carondelet	Castlewood	Cliff Cave	Emmenegger	Engelmann Woods	Faust	Greensfelder
Pyrrhopappus carolinianus				●					
Ranunculus abortivus				●	●	●			
Ranunculus fascicularis									
Ranunculus ficaria									
Ranunculus harveyi				●					
Ranunculus hispidus				●					●
Ranunculus micranthus	●			●		●	●		●
Ranunculus recurvatus									
Ranunculus sceleratus									
Ranunculus septentrionalis				●		●			
Ratibida pinnata	●	●				●	●		●
Rorippa islandica var. fernaldiana				●					
Rorippa sinuata									
Rorippa sylvestris					●				
Rosa carolina	●	●		●	●	●			●
Rosa multiflora	●								
Rosa setigera	●	●		●	●				
Rotala ramosior								●	●
Rudbeckia hirta	●	●		●	●	●	●	●	●
Rudbeckia laciniata	●			●				●	
Rudbeckia missouriensis		●				●			●
Rudbeckia triloba	●	●		●	●				●
Ruellia humilis	●			●	●				
Ruellia pedunculata		●							
Ruellia strepens	●			●					●
Rumex altissimus			●					●	
Rumex crispus	●			●	●			●	
Rumex obtusifolius				●					
Rumex verticillatus									
Sabatia angularis	●								
Sagittaria engelmanniana									
Sagittaria latifolia				●					
Sagittaria montevidensis									

Howell Island	Jefferson Barracks	Laumeier	Love	Marais Temps Clair	Mastodon	Pacific Palisades	Powder Valley	Queeny	Riverlands	Robertsville	Rockwoods	St. Stanislaus	Suson	Teszar's Woods	Valley View Glades	West Tyson	Whitecliff	Hilda J. Young
●																		
		●	●		●	●		●	●	●	●	●	●	●		●	●	
			●		●		●				●							
						●										●		
		●	●								●					●		
					●			●			●	●	●			●		
											●							
											●							●
							●									●		●
	●							●	●		●					●		
●																		
				●														
	●				●	●					●				●	●		
		●						●		●		●					●	●
					●	●					●							
	●	●	●					●	●	●	●			●		●	●	●
					●	●		●			●							
		●	●		●		●	●		●	●	●	●			●	●	●
											●				●	●		
																		●
							●			●	●		●	●		●		
				●								●	●					
			●					●	●	●			●	●				
														●				
					●										●			
		●	●					●				●						
										●								
									●									

	Babler	Bee Tree	Carondelet	Castlewood	Cliff Cave	Emmenegger	Engelmann Woods	Faust	Greensfelder
Salsola kali				●					
Samolus parviflorus									
Sanguinaria canadensis	●	●		●		●	●		●
Sanicula canadensis	●			●		●		●	●
Sanicula gregaria	●	●			●	●	●	●	●
Saponaria officinalis			●	●					
Saururus cernuus									
Saxifraga pensylvanica var. forbesii									
Scrophularia marilandica					●	●		●	●
Scutellaria incana	●					●			
Scutellaria lateriflora					●				
Scutellaria ovata	●			●	●	●	●		●
Scutellaria parvula					●				●
Senecio aureus									
Senecio glabellus									
Senecio obovatus	●			●		●			●
Seymeria macrophylla	●				●	●			
Sibara virginica		●		●			●		
Sicyos angulatus					●	●			
Sida spinosa			●	●					
Silene antirrhina									
Silene stellata					●	●	●		
Silphium integrifolium					●	●	●		●
Silphium laciniatum									●
Silphium perfoliatum	●								●
Silphium terebinthinaceum					●		●		●
Sisyrinchium albidum									
Sisyrinchium campestre	●			●		●		●	●
Sium suave									
Smilacina racemosa	●	●		●		●	●		●
Smilax tamnoides var. hispida	●			●					
Solanum americanum			●	●	●				
Solanum carolinense		●	●	●	●	●		●	

Howell Island	Jefferson Barracks	Laumeier	Love	Marais Temps Clair	Mastodon	Pacific Palisades	Powder Valley	Queeny	Riverlands	Robertsville	Rockwoods	St. Stanislaus	Suson	Teszar's Woods	Valley View Glades	West Tyson	Whitecliff	Hilda J. Young
								●					●	●				
			●		●	●	●			●	●	●	●	●		●	●	●
		●	●		●						●		●					
		●	●	●	●	●	●	●		●	●			●		●		●
					●													●
						●								●				●
				●	●			●			●	●		●		●		●
			●								●							
				●						●	●			●				
		●			●	●	●				●			●		●		
		●									●				●	●		
											●				●	●		
									●		●	●						
											●							
						●		●										
●		●		●							●			●		●		
●			●	●		●	●	●			●	●						
		●	●			●	●	●		●	●							●
	●							●	●	●	●					●		●
			●		●			●			●						●	●
		●			●						●				●			●
	●							●		●	●			●				
				●														
	●	●	●		●	●	●	●			●			●		●	●	●
●			●	●			●	●		●	●	●	●	●		●	●	
● ●			●	●	●			●		●	●	●	●	●		●		●

	Babler	Bee Tree	Carondelet	Castlewood	Cliff Cave	Emmenegger	Engelmann Woods	Faust	Greensfelder
Solanum rostratum									
Solidago altissima	●	●	●	●	●	●		●	●
Solidago buckleyi		●		●	●				
Solidago drummondii		●		●					
Solidago flexicaulis							●		
Solidago gattingeri									
Solidago gigantea				●	●	●			
Solidago hispida	●			●					●
Solidago nemoralis	●	●		●	●				●
Solidago petiolaris var. wardii	●			●					●
Solidago rigida									●
Solidago speciosa									●
Solidago ulmifolia	●	●		●	●	●			●
Sonchus asper			●	●					
Specularia biflora							●		
Specularia perfoliata	●			●		●			
Spermacoce glabra				●					
Spiranthes cernua									
Spiranthes magnicamporum									
Spiranthes tuberosa									
Stachys palustris									
Stachys tenuifolia	●			●	●				
Stellaria media	●	●	●	●	●			●	
Strophostyles helvola									
Strophostyles leiosperma									
Stylophorum diphyllum						●	●		
Stylosanthes biflora	●			●		●			
Swertia caroliniensis									
Taenidia integerrima				●		●	●		●
Taraxacum officinale	●	●	●	●	●	●	●	●	●
Tephrosia virginiana				●					
Teucrium canadense	●	●		●	●			●	
Thalictrum revolutum									

Howell Island	Jefferson Barracks	Laumeier	Love	Marais Temps Clair	Mastodon	Pacific Palisades	Powder Valley	Queeny	Riverlands	Robertsville	Rockwoods	St. Stanislaus	Suson	Teszar's Woods	Valley View Glades	West Tyson	Whitecliff	Hilda J. Young
				●														
●		●	●	●	●			●		●	●	●	●			●	●	●
											●							
					●													
											●					●		
															●			
●	●		●	●	●		●	●			●					●	●	●
											●					●		
								●			●				●	●		
											●				●			
											●							
											●				●			●
	●	●	●				●			●	●	●	●	●	●	●	●	●
				●							●							
											●					●		
		●			●	●	●			●	●				●	●		
										●				●		●		
																		●
															●			
											●							
				●														
●			●		●							●	●	●				
					●	●		●			●	●	●	●		●		●
				●				●	●									●
				●				●					●					
						●										●		
						●									●			
															●			
					●						●				●	●		
●	●	●	●		●	●	●	●	●	●	●	●	●	●		●	●	●
											●					●		
●	●	●	●	●	●			●		●	●		●					●
	●														●			

	Babler	Bee Tree	Carondelet	Castlewood	Cliff Cave	Emmenegger	Engelmann Woods	Faust	Greensfelder
Thaspium barbinode							●		
Thaspium trifoliatum var. flavum	●								
Thlaspi arvense	●	●					●	●	
Thlaspi perfoliatum	●			●			●		●
Torilis japonica	●	●		●				●	●
Tradescantia ohiensis	●		●	●	●	●			●
Tragopogon dubius	●			●		●		●	
Trifolium campestre	●	●		●				●	●
Trifolium pratense	●		●	●	●				
Trifolium repens	●	●		●	●		●	●	●
Trillium flexipes	●						●		
Trillium recurvatum	●	●		●		●	●	●	●
Trillium viride				●			●		
Triosteum angustifolium						●			
Triosteum aurantiacum				●					
Triosteum perfoliatum	●			●	●				●
Typha latifolia		●	●	●					
Urtica dioica var. procera	●			●	●	●		●	
Uvularia grandiflora	●	●		●	●	●	●		●
Valerianella radiata	●			●					
Veratrum woodii							●		
Verbascum blattaria	●			●					
Verbascum thapsus	●			●	●				
Verbena bracteata					●				
Verbena canadensis				●		●	●		●
Verbena hastata									
Verbena simplex					●				
Verbena stricta				●					
Verbena urticifolia	●	●		●	●			●	
Verbesina alternifolia	●	●	●	●	●	●			●
Verbesina helianthoides	●	●							●
Verbesina virginica	●			●	●				
Vernonia altissima	●	●							

Howell Island	Jefferson Barracks	Laumeier	Love	Marais Temps Clair	Mastodon	Pacific Palisades	Powder Valley	Queeny	Riverlands	Robertsville	Rockwoods	St. Stanislaus	Suson	Teszar's Woods	Valley View Glades	West Tyson	Whitecliff	Hilda J. Young
		•																
						•					•	•		•		•	•	•
						•			•		•		•					•
	•	•		•	•					•	•		•	•				
	•	•			•	•					•					•	•	•
•	•	•	•	•	•	•		•		•	•	•	•			•	•	•
		•	•		•					•	•	•				•	•	•
								•			•							
	•	•				•	•		•	•	•	•	•			•		
		•								•			•		•			
		•																
					•		•				•					•		•
	•								•	•							•	•
•	•			•														
			•			•	•				•				•	•		
						•									•	•		
															•			•
•	•			•		•					•					•	•	•
	•		•							•						•	•	
				•		•					•					•		•
•			•					•										
											•							
										•					•			
•	•	•	•		•		•	•		•	•		•				•	•
		•		•			•			•	•				•	•	•	•
	•									•	•				•	•	•	•
										•								
	•	•		•						•								

	Babler	Bee Tree	Carondelet	Castlewood	Cliff Cave	Emmenegger	Engelmann Woods	Faust	Greensfelder
Vernonia baldwinii	●	●		●	●	●	●		
Vernonia crinita				●					
Vernonia fasciculata									
Vernonia missurica			●	●					
Veronica arvensis	●		●	●	●		●	●	
Veronica hederaefolia									
Veronica peregrina				●		●			●
Veronica polita	●	●							
Veronicastrum virginicum									
Vicia sativa				●					
Vicia villosa		●						●	
Vinca minor	●	●			●		●		
Viola papilionacea		●	●	●			●		
Viola pedata var. lineariloba		●		●		●	●		●
Viola pedata var. pedata		●		●		●	●		●
Viola pensylvanica	●			●		●	●		●
Viola rafinesquii	●	●		●			●		●
Viola sororia	●	●		●		●	●		●
Viola striata	●			●			●		●
Viola triloba						●	●		●
Xanthium strumarium				●	●			●	●
Yucca smalliana									
Zizia aurea				●		●			●

A species/location checklist grid. Column headers (left to right):

Howell Island	Jefferson Barracks	Laumeier	Love	Marais Temps Clair	Mastodon	Pacific Palisades	Powder Valley	Queeny	Riverlands	Robertsville	Rockwoods	St. Stanislaus	Suson	Teszar's Woods	Valley View Glades	West Tyson	Whitecliff	Hilda J. Young
	●	●			●		●	●		●						●	●	
				●														
										●			●					
		●						●			●		●					
													●					
		●																
		●											●	●			●	
	●	●									●					●		
								●										
																		●
												●						
			●			●				●	●	●						
										●					●	●		
																●		
		●				●				●	●	●	●			●		
					●	●				●	●		●			●		●
		●	●		●	●	●			●	●	●				●	●	●
		●	●			●		●		●	●	●	●			●		●
		●							●	●	●							
●				●		●						●		●			●	●
											●	●						
					●						●							

Botanical Terms

Alternate Arranged so that only one leaf occurs at any given position on the stem.

Anther The pollen-bearing part of the stamen, borne at the top of the filament.

Basal Rising directly from the base of the stem.

Blade The expanded part of a leaf or petal.

Bract A reduced or modified leaf, usually growing at the base of a flower.

Bud An unexpanded flower.

Bulb A subterranean enlarged leaf bud with fleshy scales.

Calyx The outer circle of floral parts consisting of sepals.

Corm The enlarged, solid, bulblike base of a stem.

Corolla The petals, collectively.

Disk flower *See* Head.

Entire Unbroken by toothing, lobing, or division.

Filament The anther-bearing stalk of a stamen.

Glabrous Not hairy.

Glaucous Covered with a whitish substance, a "bloom" that can be rubbed off.

Hastate Shaped like an arrowhead but with basal lobes pointed outward at a wide angle.

Head A tightly packed cluster containing strap-shaped ray flowers and/or tubular disk flowers. The term is used in referring to the flowers of the Daisy family, which may have one or more of the basic parts depicted below.

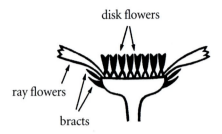

Inflorescence The flowering part of a plant and especially its form of arrangement.

Involucral Pertaining to an involucre.

Involucre A collection of small bracts or leaves surrounding the base of a flower cluster or the head of a single flower.

Lanceolate Several times longer than wide, broadest at the base and narrowed toward the apex.

Opposite Used to refer to leaves that are paired at the nodes.

Ovary The section of the pistil that contains what becomes the seed after fertilization.

Panicle A compound form of flower grouping in which individual flowers occur on side branches off the main stalk.

Pedicel The stalk of an individual flower that is a part of a cluster.

Peduncle The stem of a solitary flower when that flower is the only member of the inflorescence.

Petiole The stalk of a leaf.

Pistil The female part of a flower consisting of stigma, style, and ovary.

Pollen The grains in the anther containing the male element.

Raceme A long inflorescence of individually stalked flowers arising from a common axis.

Ray flower *See* Head.

Rhizome A creeping stem underground or at ground level.

Sepal A sterile, sometimes petal-like and sometimes leaflike, division of the calyx.

Sessile Without a stalk.

Stalk The stem of a flower or leaf.

Stamen One of the pollen-bearing organs of the flower; composed of an anther and a filament.

Standard The upper, broad, primarily erect petal of a flower in the Leguminosae (Fabaceae) family.

Stigma The uppermost end of the pistil; the part to receive the pollen.

Style The part of the pistil bearing the stigma.

Tuber A short, thick, usually underground stem having numerous buds called "eyes."

Umbel A flower cluster in which all the individual flower stalks radiate from a common point.

Whorled Arranged in a circle around the stem.

References of Interest

Denison, Edgar. 1989. *Missouri Wildflowers.* 4th ed. Jefferson City: Missouri Department of Conservation. 314 pp. Contains color photographs and black-and-white line drawings.

Eisendrath, Erna R. 1978. *Missouri Wildflowers of the St. Louis Area.* St. Louis: Missouri Botanical Garden. 390 pp. Contains black-and-white line drawings. Fairly complete for the plants covered in this book.

Steyermark, Julian A. 1963. *Flora of Missouri.* Ames: Iowa State University Press. 1,725 pp. Out of print but well worth locating.

Summers, Bill. 1981. *Missouri Orchids.* Jefferson City: Missouri Department of Conservation. 92 pp. Contains color photographs and black-and-white line drawings.

Yatskievych, George, and Joanna Turner. 1990. *Catalogue of the Flora of Missouri.* St. Louis: Missouri Botanical Garden. 345 pp. A checklist of the currently used names of the state's flora.

Acknowledgments

Endless appreciation is extended

—to George Yatskievych, who shared his vast botanical knowledge, seasoned with a dash of wry humor, by answering a variety of questions posed to him during the writing of this text;

—to Kay Yatskievych, for helping me to organize my thoughts and plans for the project into a concise program of action;

—to John E. Molyneaux, who gave generously of his time in two dimensions: first, by working with me in the field as photographic adviser/assistant; second, after Arthur died, by accompanying me on the final expeditions to check the accuracy of my directions for finding each featured wildflower;

—to Reverend James Sullivan and other members of the Webster Groves Nature Study Society–Botany Group for the botanical knowledge shared on field trips;

—to Bill Summers for assistance in locating plant specimens in the herbarium of the Missouri Botanical Garden;

—to Dee Dee Lafata, whose nimble fingers flew over the word-processor keys spelling out scientific names of incredible diversity;

—to Albert J. Haller, my husband and attorney, for help in making a final selection of slides for use in the book and for expert legal advice as needed;

—to Christopher K. Haller, my son, a graphic designer, for the well-designed sample layouts provided for submission with the manuscript;

—to Debra L. Haller, my daughter, a television writer/producer, for long-distance encouragement and advice from her home in Connecticut;

—and to my parents, Frieda and Frank Kratoville, for providing an atmosphere for growth of intellectual curiosity and appreciation for the natural environment.

Index

About the Author

Photo by Suzy Gorman

An amateur botanist, **Karen S. Haller** has been affiliated with numerous nature societies and has held a number of offices, including President of the Missouri Native Plant Association. She is the author of various nature articles and was a contributing photographer for several books.